Early United States

HARCOURT BRACE SOCIAL STUDIES

ACTIVITY BOOK

HARCOURT BRACE & COMPANY

Orlando Atlanta Austin Boston San Francisco Chicago Dallas
New York Toronto London

Visit The Learning Site at http://www.hbschool.com

Copyright © by Harcourt Brace & Company

All rights reserved. No part of this publication may be reproduced or transmitted in any form or by any means, electronic or mechanical, including photocopy, recording, or any information storage and retrieval system, without permission in writing from the publisher.

Permission is hereby granted to individual teachers using the corresponding student's textbook or kit as the major vehicle for regular classroom instruction to photocopy complete pages from this publication in classroom quantities for instructional use and not for resale.

Duplication of this work other than by individual classroom teachers under the conditions specified above requires a license. To order a license to duplicate this work in greater than classroom quantities, contact Customer Service, Harcourt Brace & Company, 6277 Sea Harbor Drive, Orlando, Florida 32887-6777. Telephone: 1-800-225-5425. Fax: 1-800-874-6418 or 407-352-3445.

HARCOURT BRACE and Quill Design is a registered trademark of Harcourt Brace & Company.

For permission to reprint copyrighted material, grateful acknowledgment is made to the following sources:

Chelsea House Publishers, a division of Main Line Book Co.: From "If You Miss Me from the Back of the Bus" in *Songs of Protest and Civil Rights,* compiled by Jerry Silverman. Lyrics copyright © 1992 by Chelsea House Publishers, a division of Main Line Book Co.

Dutton Children's Books, a division of Penguin Putnam Inc.: From *Immigrant Kids* by Russell Freedman. Text copyright © 1980 by Russell Freedman.

The McGraw-Hill Companies: From book #60660 *The Log of Christopher Columbus* by Robert H. Fuson. Text copyright 1987 by Robert H. Fuson. Original English language edition published by International Marine Publishing Company, Camden, ME.

Printed in the United States of America

ISBN 0-15-310308-6

The activities in this book reinforce or extend social studies concepts and skills in **EARLY UNITED STATES**. There is one activity for each lesson and skill. Reproductions of the activity pages appear with answers in the Teacher's Edition.

CONTENTS

UNIT 1

Chapter 1

Lesson 1	A Native American Belief	1
Skill	How to Compare Map Projections	2–3
Lesson 2	Think Like an Archaeologist	4
Skill	How to Identify Patterns on Time Lines	5
Lesson 3	Preserving Native American Artifacts	6
Chapter Review	The First Americans	7

Chapter 2

Lesson 1	Two Northwest Coast Indian Canoes	8
Lesson 2	Learning About Kachinas	9
Lesson 3	The Importance of the Buffalo	10
Lesson 4	Hiawatha & Longfellow Make History	11
Skill	How to Identify Causes and Effects	12
Lesson 5	Unlocking the Mystery of Mayan Numbers	13
Chapter Review	Indians of North America	14

UNIT 2

Chapter 3

Lesson 1	A Viking Ship	15
Lesson 2	Marco Polo and the Riches of Asia	16
Lesson 3	The Log of Christopher Columbus	17
Skill	How to Use Latitude and Longitude	18
Lesson 4	The Costs of Exploration	19
Skill	How to Form a Logical Conclusion	20
Chapter Review	The Age of Exploration	21

Chapter 4

Lesson 1	A Day in Tenochtitlán	22
Lesson 2	Estéban in Time and Place	23
Lesson 3	Do You Speak Spanish?	24
Skill	How to Use a Map to Show Movement	25

Lesson 4	Preparing Furs for Trade	26
Lesson 5	Harvest Festivals	27
Skill	How to Read Parallel Time Lines	28
Chapter Review	Encounters in the Americas	29

UNIT 3

Chapter 5

Lesson 1	Comparing Spanish Missions	30
Lesson 2	A Taste of Louisiana	31
Lesson 3	The Routes of Three Colonists	32
Lesson 4	The Middle Colonies	33
Lesson 5	Comparing the Colonies	34–35
Skill	How to Classify Information	36
Chapter Review	Europeans Settle Throughout North America	37

Chapter 6

Lesson 1	Having a Whale of a Time	38
Skill	How to Read a Circle Graph	39
Lesson 2	Looking at Life in the Southern Colonies	40
Lesson 3	Tooling Around the Frontier	41
Skill	How to Use a Product Map to Make Generalizations	42
Chapter Review	Life in the British Colonies	43

UNIT 4

Chapter 7

Lesson 1	Historical Events of the 1700s	44
Skill	How to Use a Historical Map	45
Lesson 2	Understanding Proverbs in *Poor Richard's Almanack*	46
Lesson 3	Events Leading to Revolution	47
Skill	How to Make Economic Choices	48
Chapter Review	Differences Divide Britain and Its Colonies	49

Chapter 8

Lesson 1	The Redcoats Are Coming!	50
Skill	How to Read a Political Cartoon	51
Lesson 2	A Woman Printed the Declaration of Independence	52
Skill	How to Learn from Pictures	53

Lesson 3	Americans Take Sides	54
Lesson 4	Characterize Patriots	55
Lesson 5	Which Event Happened First?	56
Chapter Review	The War for Independence	57

UNIT 5

Chapter 9

Lesson 1	Articles of Confederation	58
Lesson 2	Who Was There?	59
Skill	How to Figure Travel Time and Distance	60
Lesson 3	Who Has the Power?	61
Skill	How to Compromise to Resolve Conflicts	62
Lesson 4	Who Does What in the Government?	63
Lesson 5	Constitutional Footnotes	64
Chapter Review	The Constitution	65

Chapter 10

Lesson 1	The Maze of Ratification	66
Lesson 2	Counting the Amendments	67
Lesson 3	Who's in Office?	68
Skill	How to Learn from a Document	69
Chapter Review	A New Government Begins	70

UNIT 6

Chapter 11

Lesson 1	Blazing a Trail West	71
Lesson 2	Follow Their Footsteps	72
Lesson 3	The Growth of Nationalism	73
Skill	How to Predict a Likely Outcome	74
Lesson 4	The Flag Was Still There	75
Chapter Review	On the Move	76

Chapter 12

Lesson 1	Inventors and Their Inventions	77
Lesson 2	The Trail of Tears	78
Lesson 3	The Oregon Trail	79
Skill	How to Use Relief and Elevation Maps	80
Lesson 4	Seneca Falls	81
Skill	How to Use a Double-Bar Graph	82–83
Chapter Review	The Way West	84

UNIT 7

Chapter 13

Lesson 1	A Tale of Two Regions, 1860	85
Skill	How to Use Graphs to Identify Trends	86
Lesson 2	The Life and Times of a Slave	87
Lesson 3	"Bleeding Kansas"	88
Lesson 4	Why Did South Carolina Secede?	89
Skill	How to Make a Thoughtful Decision	90
Chapter Review	Background to the Conflict	91

Chapter 14

Lesson 1	The Bonnie Blue Flag	92
Lesson 2	The Emancipation Proclamation	93
Lesson 3	Civil War Horses	94
Skill	How to Compare Maps with Different Scales	95
Lesson 4	It's in the Bag!	96
Chapter Review	Civil War and Reconstruction	97

UNIT 8

Chapter 15

Lesson 1	Famous Entrepreneurs	98
Skill	How to Use a Time Zone Map	99–100
Lesson 2	Duke Ellington	101
Lesson 3	Organizing Resources	102
Lesson 4	School Days	103
Skill	How to Solve a Problem	104
Chapter Review	A Changing America	105

Chapter 16

Lesson 1	Immigration	106
Skill	How to Compare Information on Graphs	107
Lesson 2	An African American Portrait	108
Lesson 3	Sing About Civil Rights	109
Skill	How to Act as a Responsible Citizen	110
Lesson 4	An American Song	111
Chapter Review	The Promise of America	112

NAME _____ DATE _____

A Native American Belief

Understand Oral History

DIRECTIONS: Read the following quotation. It describes what some Native Americans believe about their origins and their rights. Then answer the questions that follow.

> "When we were created we were given our ground to live on and from this time these were our rights. This is all true. We were put here by the Creator—I was not brought from a foreign country and did not come here. I was put here by the Creator."
>
> —*Chief Weninock, Yakima,* 1915

1. According to this quotation, where did the first Americans come from? _____

2. Which sentence in the passage disagrees with the theory that the first Americans came across the Bering Strait? _____

3. In the passage, what does "these were our rights" refer to? _____

4. What can you conclude about Native Americans' beliefs about land rights? _____

5. Why do you think Chief Weninock felt that he needed to state "This is all true"? _____

Use after reading Chapter 1, Lesson 1, pages 47–53.

NAME _____ DATE _____

HOW TO COMPARE MAP Projections

Only a globe can show exact shape, size, direction, and distance on the Earth. Cartographers try to show these four features of the Earth on a flat map as exactly as possible, but all map projections have distortions.

Apply Map and Globe Skills

DIRECTIONS: Study the map projections on this page and the following page. Then read each statement on the next page. Decide whether the statement applies to a Mercator projection, to a Mollweide projection, or to both projections. Place a check on the correct line or lines.

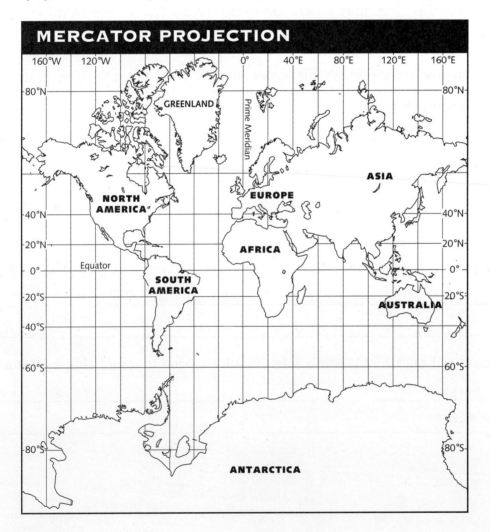

(continued)

2 ACTIVITY BOOK   Use after reading Chapter 1, Skill Lesson, pages 56–57.

NAME _____ DATE _____

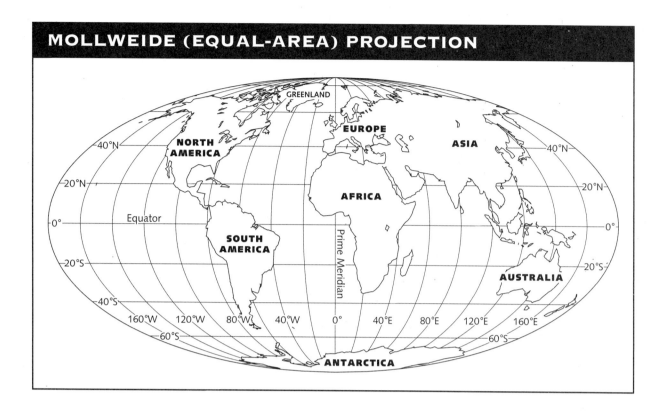

Mercator   Mollweide

_____ _____ 1. Shows the seven continents.

_____ _____ 2. Shows the curved feature of the Earth.

_____ _____ 3. Uses straight lines for all lines of latitude and longitude.

_____ _____ 4. Shows all lines of latitude and longitude at right angles to each other.

_____ _____ 5. Uses a straight line for the equator.

_____ _____ 6. Uses a straight line for the prime meridian.

_____ _____ 7. Shows meridians intersecting at the top and bottom of the map.

_____ _____ 8. Shows parallels NOT intersecting.

_____ _____ 9. Uses straight lines to show latitude.

_____ _____ 10. Shows sizes of places true to scale.

_____ _____ 11. Shows Greenland as about the same size as Africa.

_____ _____ 12. Uses curved lines to show longitude.

Use after reading Chapter 1, Skill Lesson, pages 56–57.

NAME _____ DATE _____

THINK LIKE an Archaeologist

An archaeologist uses artifacts to learn about past cultures. Archaeologists are trained to find clues from artifacts in order to learn about a culture. They are also trained to know what clues artifacts do NOT give.

Interpret Visuals

DIRECTIONS: Study the following artifacts. Then write the name of the artifact that best answers the questions below.

Club
Made from wood.
Used for hunting.

Bone Needle
Made from an animal bone splinter. Used to sew hides into clothing and tents.

Basket
Woven in different ways for different purposes. Used for gathering, preparing, and storing food.

Pottery
Made by coiling thin rolls of clay on top of one another. Used for storage and cooking.

Atlatl
Spear-throwing weapon made of wood.
Used for hunting.

1. Which artifact would have been the best to use to hunt the woolly mammoth?
   _____

2. Which artifact shows that Native Americans made clothing? _____

3. Which two artifacts show that the Native Americans were food gatherers and farmers?
   _____

4. Which three artifacts show that the Native Americans worked with crafts?
   _____

5. Which two artifacts could have been used for cooking? _____

NAME _____ DATE _____

HOW TO IDENTIFY Patterns on Time Lines

Apply Chart and Graph Skills

DIRECTIONS: Each of the six statements that follow tells how many years ago an event occurred. For each one, change the number of years shown to a calendar date using B.C. To change, or convert, from number of years ago to a B.C. date, subtract 2,000. Write these dates in the spaces provided. Then write the question number of each event above the correct date on the time line.

1. The land bridge theory says the first people arrived in the Americas about 12,000 years ago. _____

2. Artifacts from about 13,000 years ago have been found in Monte Verde, Chile. _____

3. Clovis points were first made about 11,600 years ago. _____

4. Giant mammals became extinct in the Americas about 10,000 years ago. _____

5. The last Ice Age ended about 10,000 years ago. _____

6. Farming was practiced in central Mexico 7,000 years ago. _____

| 11,000 B.C. | 10,000 B.C. | 9000 B.C. | 8000 B.C. | 7000 B.C. | 6000 B.C. | 5000 B.C. | 4000 B.C. |

Use after reading Chapter 1, Skill Lesson, pages 64–65.

NAME _____ DATE _____

Preserving Native American Artifacts

Read Information in a Table

DIRECTIONS: The following table lists some of the best-preserved sites of early Native American settlements in North America. Use the information in the table to answer the questions that follow.

SITES OF NATIVE AMERICAN ARTIFACTS

NAME OF SITE	LOCATION	SIZE	FAST FACTS
Chaco Canyon National Historical Park	Bloomfield, New Mexico	33 sq miles (85 sq km)	Contains 18 major ruins dating from about A.D. 920 to A.D. 1130. Pueblo Bonito (meaning "beautiful town") was one of the largest Native American apartment-style houses. It was about 5 stories high, had 800 rooms and 32 circular kivas, and housed more than 1,200 people.
Effigy Mounds National Monument	Near Marquette, Iowa	2 sq miles (5 sq km)	Has burial mounds shaped like birds and animals. The Mound Builder people were active from about 1000 B.C. to about A.D. 1500.
Mesa Verde National Park	Southwestern Colorado	53,036 acres	Occupied from about A.D. 1 to about A.D. 1300. One pueblo, the Cliff Palace, held up to 1,000 people and had 200 rooms. Abandoned about two centuries before Europeans arrived in the Americas.
Petrified Forest National Park	Near Holbrook, Arizona	93,493 acres	Occupied A.D. 500 and remained occupied for 1,000 years. Preserves Native American petroglyphs (rock carvings) and prehistoric ruins.

1. At which site can you see burial mounds shaped like animals?

   _____

2. At which site can you find one of the largest apartment-style houses?

   _____

3. At which site can you see petroglyphs? _____

4. Which site is not located in the southwestern part of the United States?

   _____

5. Which site is the oldest? _____

NAME _____ DATE _____

The First AMERICANS

Connect Main Ideas

DIRECTIONS: Use this organizer to show how the environment affected the lives of early people. Write three details to support each main idea.

The First Americans

The Search for Early Peoples

The environment affected the ways early peoples moved from place to place.

1. _____
2. _____
3. _____

Ancient Indians

The ancient Indians changed their ways of life as the environment changed.

1. _____
_____
_____
_____
2. _____
_____
_____
_____
3. _____
_____

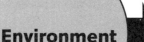

Early Civilizations

Early peoples living in different parts of the Americas had different ways of life.

1. _____
_____
_____
_____
2. _____
_____
_____
_____
3. _____
_____

Use after reading Chapter 1, pages 46–73.

NAME _____ DATE _____

TWO Northwest Coast Indian Canoes

The Northwest Coast Indians used dugout canoes with two different shapes. One type of canoe was built by the Haida. The other was built by the Nootka. Although the canoes were shaped differently, the methods and materials used to make them were the same. Both dugouts were made of cedar. The largest canoes were more than 60 feet (18 m) long and as much as 8 feet (2 m) wide.

Compare Diagrams

DIRECTIONS: Compare the diagrams of the two types of canoes. Then answer the questions that follow.

HAIDA

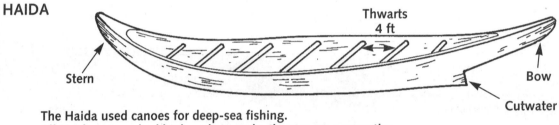

The Haida used canoes for deep-sea fishing.
All Haida canoes had high ends to make them more seaworthy.

NOOTKA

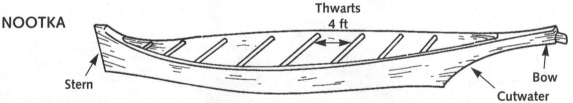

The Nootka used canoes for whaling.
All Nootka canoes had a flat strip on the bottom to keep them upright during whale hunts.

1. For what purpose was the Haida canoe used? _____

2. For what purpose was the Nootka canoe used? _____

3. Look at the bows, or the front ends, of the two canoes. How are they different?
   _____

4. Now compare the sterns, or the back ends, of the two canoes. How are they different?
   _____

5. The thwarts, or braces, that run across the canoes held the canoes' sides in place.

   How far apart are the thwarts? _____

NAME _____ DATE _____

Learning About Kachinas

Compare Visuals

DIRECTIONS: Study the drawings and descriptions of the three kachinas. Then answer the questions that follow.

Sun Kachina

Visits Hopi villages during the bean-planting ceremony. Appeals to the sun for health, happiness, long life, and good crops.

Clown Kachina

Appears during most ceremonies to entertain the crowd. Performs acrobatics, tells jokes, and leads games. Is noisy and silly.

Kachina Mother

Leads the bean-planting ceremony. Is actually a male performer.

1. Which kachina is a spirit of nature? _____

2. How can you tell one kind of kachina from another? _____
   _____

3. Which part of the Sun Kachina's costume represents the sun?
   _____

4. What makes the Clown Kachina's costume different from the other kachinas' costumes?
   _____
   _____

5. Which kachina do you think would play the most important role at the bean-planting ceremony? Explain. _____

Use after reading Chapter 2, Lesson 2, pages 81–85.

NAME _____ DATE _____

The Importance of the BUFFALO

The buffalo played an important part in the history of our country. As long as the buffalo roamed the Great Plains, the Plains Indians grew in number and strength. The people of the Plains hunted the buffalo for food and used other parts of the animal to make clothing, tools, weapons, and other products.

Interpret Visuals

DIRECTIONS: Study the drawings below, which show the most common buffalo products. Then answer the questions that follow.

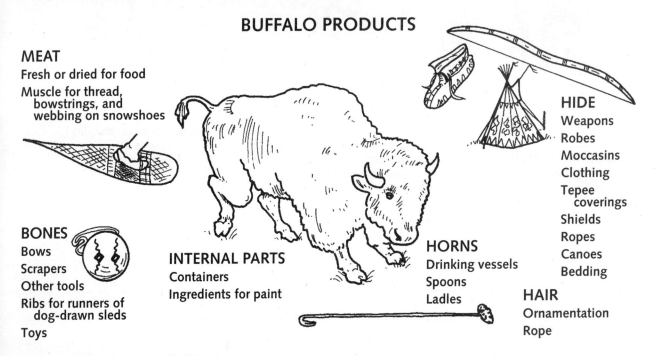

BUFFALO PRODUCTS

MEAT
Fresh or dried for food
Muscle for thread, bowstrings, and webbing on snowshoes

BONES
Bows
Scrapers
Other tools
Ribs for runners of dog-drawn sleds
Toys

INTERNAL PARTS
Containers
Ingredients for paint

HORNS
Drinking vessels
Spoons
Ladles

HIDE
Weapons
Robes
Moccasins
Clothing
Tepee coverings
Shields
Ropes
Canoes
Bedding

HAIR
Ornamentation
Rope

1. What did the Plains Indians make from the internal parts of the buffalo?

_____

2. Which three parts of the buffalo were used to make different kinds of weapons?

_____

3. Which part of the buffalo was used to make housing for the Plains Indians?

_____

4. Which part of the buffalo do you think made the most useful products?

_____

10 ACTIVITY BOOK   Use after reading Chapter 2, Lesson 3, pages 86–91.

NAME _____ DATE _____

Hiawatha & Longfellow Make History

Interpret Historical Literature

DIRECTIONS: Study the information about Hiawatha and the lines from Longfellow's poem. Then answer the questions.

    Hiawatha, an Onondaga chief, worked hard for peace. In the late 1500s, he persuaded war-weary tribes of the Iroquois nation to stop fighting one another. They united in peace by forming what became known as the Iroquois League.

    Hiawatha was believed to have been a shaman, or a religious leader and healer who calls upon the gods to grant the people special favors. He was said to have magical powers. Native American stories describe Hiawatha as a great teacher who taught valuable lessons about farming, hunting, canoeing, medicine, nature, and the arts.

    Many years after Hiawatha's death, the stories about Hiawatha inspired Henry Wadsworth Longfellow to write the poem "The Song of Hiawatha." It took Longfellow from June 1854 to March 1855 to write it! You may recognize some verses from this lengthy poem. The lines that follow are from the section about Hiawatha's fasting, a time when he deliberately ate very little or nothing at all.

> "You shall hear how Hiawatha
> Prayed and fasted in the forest,
> Not for greater skill in hunting,
> Not for greater craft in fishing,
> Not for triumphs in the battle,
> And renown [fame] among the warriors,
> But for profit of the people,
> For advantage of the nations."

1. What was Hiawatha's major accomplishment? _____
_____

2. What is a shaman? _____
_____

3. Why do you think Longfellow was inspired to write a poem about Hiawatha?
_____

4. According to the poem, what was the purpose of Hiawatha's fasting?
_____
_____

NAME _____ DATE _____

HOW TO IDENTIFY CAUSES and EFFECTS

Most scientists believe the first Americans crossed over a land bridge from Asia to the Americas. This great migration lasted thousands of years. What was the cause of this great migration? What were the effects?

Apply Critical Thinking Skills

DIRECTIONS: Use the information in Unit 1 about the great migration to complete the following flow chart. Use the flow chart on page 97 of your textbook as a guide.

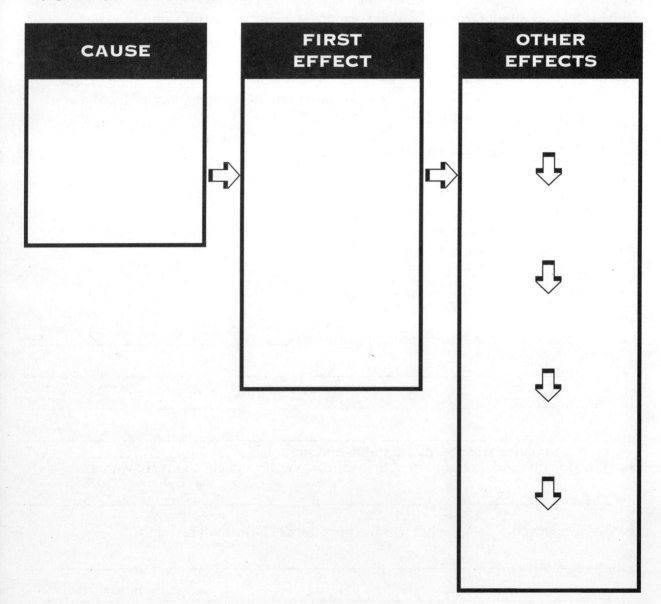

12 ACTIVITY BOOK   Use after reading Chapter 2, Skill Lesson, page 97.

NAME _____ DATE _____

Unlocking the Mystery of MAYAN NUMBERS

The Mayas built one of the most well-developed civilizations in the Americas. Their civilization was so highly developed that they had a system for writing and recording time. The Mayas' time system was based on their number system, which used three basic symbols. A shell stood for zero, a dot stood for one, and a bar stood for five.

Recognize Patterns

DIRECTIONS: Study the diagram that shows how the Mayas used three basic symbols in their number system. Then, write the Arabic numerals we would use to write the number that each Mayan symbol or group of symbols represents.

0	1	3
5	11	17

1. ___ • • •
2. ___ • • • •
3. ___ • • • ═
4. ___ ──
5. ___ • • • ─
6. ___ • • ═
7. ___ • • ═
8. ___ ═
9. ___ • • • • ═

10. Write your age using the Mayan number system. _____

Use after reading Chapter 2, Lesson 5, pages 98–103.

ACTIVITY BOOK 13

NAME _____ DATE _____

Indians OF NORTH AMERICA

Connect Main Ideas

DIRECTIONS: Use this organizer to show the diversity of the ways of life of the American Indians. Write three examples for each cultural region.

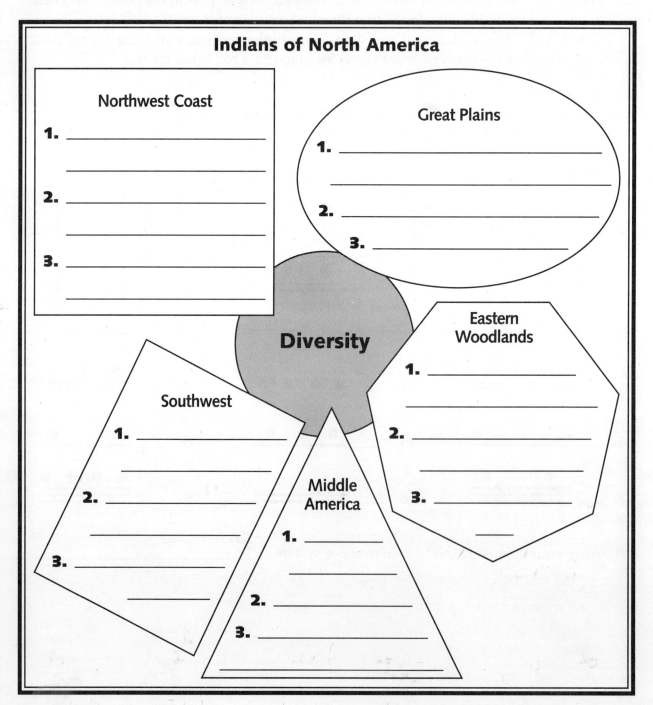

14 ACTIVITY BOOK

NAME _____ DATE _____

The Log of CHRISTOPHER COLUMBUS

Columbus's log shows that he was aware of more than just the sea. His original log, which was given to the king and queen of Spain, was lost. But a copy, passed down from Columbus to his sons and grandson, is our link to Columbus's original log.

Interpret Primary Sources

DIRECTIONS: Read the following accounts from Columbus's log. Then answer the questions that follow.

> *Thursday, 20 September, 1492.* Very early this morning three little birds flew over the ship, singing as they went, and flew away as the sun rose. This was a comforting thought, for unlike the large waterbirds, these little birds could not have come from far off.
>
> *Sunday, 23 September, 1492.* I saw a dove, a tern, another small river bird and some white birds. . . . The crew is still grumbling about the wind. When I get a wind from the southwest or west it is inconstant, and that, along with a flat sea, has led the men to believe that we will never get home.
>
> *Monday, 24 September, 1492.* I am having serious trouble with the crew. . . . They have said that it is insanity . . . on their part to risk their lives following the madness of a foreigner. . . . I am told by a few trusted men (and these are few in number!) that if I persist in going onward, the best course of action will be to throw me into the sea some night.
>
> (Reprinted by permission of The McGraw-Hill Companies.)

1. Why was Columbus comforted when he saw the little birds?

_____

2. Use context clues to find the definition of *inconstant*. In your own words, what does inconstant mean? _____

_____

3. Why would an inconstant wind make the crew believe that they would not get home?

_____

4. Imagine being on board Columbus's ship. On a separate sheet of paper, rewrite the three entries from Columbus's log as though you were one of the crew.

Use after reading Chapter 3, Lesson 3, pages 130–135.

NAME _____   DATE _____

HOW TO USE Latitude and Longitude

Columbus was an experienced sailor when he began his search for a new water route to Asia. His first voyage after settling in Portugal appears to have been in early 1477. The map shows some of his other early voyages.

Apply Map and Globe Skills

DIRECTIONS: On the map, study the voyages Columbus made before 1492. Then complete the activities.

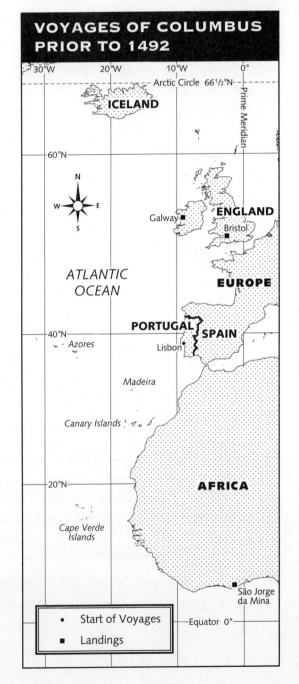

VOYAGES OF COLUMBUS PRIOR TO 1492

1. Columbus set sail from Lisbon on each of his early voyages. Circle this city on the map.

2. What is Lisbon's location? Use longitude and latitude in your answer.

   _____

3. Put an **X** through Columbus's southernmost landing.

4. Draw a box around the landings that are located between 40°N and 60°N latitude.

5. Historians believe that Columbus landed in Iceland in 1477. At that time most people thought Iceland's northernmost point was at 63°N latitude. Columbus's landing proved otherwise. On the map locate Iceland's northernmost point and write the correct latitude in the space provided.

   _____

6. What name do we give this special parallel? _____

7. Between which two meridians were Columbus's landings? _____

18 ACTIVITY BOOK

NAME _____ DATE _____

The Costs of EXPLORATION

Compare Costs

DIRECTIONS: Read the information below and study the comparison table. Then complete the activities that follow.

COSTS OF COLUMBUS'S VOYAGE OF DISCOVERY

	MARAVEDIS	U.S. DOLLARS*
Salaries of all officers	268,000	34,840
Wages of all sailors	252,000	32,760
Maintenance	319,680	41,558
Rental cost, *Santa Maria*	172,800	22,464
Furnishings, arms, trading supplies	155,062	20,158
Total Expenses	**1,167,542**	**151,780**

*maravedis × $0.13 = U.S. dollars

How can we understand the costs of Columbus's voyage when prices and values have changed over the centuries? One way is to compare costs by using the value of gold. The maravedi was a copper coin used in Spain in the 1400s. Each maravedi would have about a value of just over 13 cents. The table at the right shows the costs of the first voyage in maravedis and United States dollars.

1. Put a dollar sign ($) next to the most expensive part of the voyage. Then put an **X** next to the least expensive part of the voyage.

2. Compare the salaries of the officers and the wages of the sailors. Did it cost more to pay the officers or the sailors? Circle the one that cost more.

3. Columbus offered a reward of 10,000 maravedis to the first person to sight land. What is this amount in U.S. dollars? _____

4. The average yearly wage of a sailor on Columbus's voyage was 3,000 maravedis, or $390. Columbus's yearly salary was 50,000 maravedis, or $6,500. If you were a sailor on Columbus's voyage, considering your average yearly wages, would the 10,000 maravedi reward make you want to continue to look for land? (Columbus eventually claimed the reward for himself.) Explain. _____

Use after reading Chapter 3, Lesson 4, pages 138–144.

NAME _____ DATE _____

HOW TO FORM A Logical Conclusion

Columbus died believing that he had reached Asia. Other explorers, however, proved him wrong. Among those explorers were Vespucci, Balboa, and Magellan. These explorers found new facts to prove that Columbus had landed on a different continent.

Apply Critical Thinking Skills

DIRECTIONS: Decide which explorer could have made each statement below. In the space provided, write a V for Vespucci, a B for Balboa, or an M for Magellan. Then draw an X through any statement that does not support the conclusion that these explorers had landed on a different continent.

1. _____ I found a new way of measuring east and west distances on a map.
2. _____ I was Portuguese, sailing under the Spanish flag.
3. _____ I was killed in a fight on the Philippine Islands.
4. _____ I learned that I had sailed more than three times as far as Columbus thought he had sailed.
5. _____ Many of my crew died of scurvy and hunger.
6. _____ I found a huge ocean on the western side of what Columbus had thought was Asia.
7. _____ I climbed a mountain peak on the Isthmus of Panama.
8. _____ I studied Ptolemy's work and found that if Asia were as far east as Columbus had thought, it would cover half the Earth.
9. _____ In the areas I explored, I saw no evidence of what Marco Polo had seen in Asia.
10. _____ I found that you could reach Asia by sailing west around the world.
11. _____ I supported Vespucci's findings by crossing the Isthmus of Panama.
12. _____ My ships sailed for more than three months across the Pacific.
13. _____ My exploring party included Spanish and African soldiers.
14. _____ I set sail in September 1519.

NAME _____ DATE _____

The Age of Exploration

Connect Main Ideas

DIRECTIONS: Use this organizer to show how new information helped Europeans gain knowledge and explore the unknown. Write three details for each lesson.

The Age of Exploration

A Legendary Land
1. _____
2. _____
3. _____

↓ New Information

Background to European Exploration
1. _____
2. _____
3. _____

↓ New Information

I, Columbus: My Journal 1492–1493
1. _____
2. _____
3. _____

↓ New Information

Early Voyages of Exploration
1. _____
2. _____
3. _____

Use after reading Chapter 3, pages 118–147.

ACTIVITY BOOK 21

NAME _____ DATE _____

A Day in TENOCHTITLÁN

What was it like to live in the Aztec capital of Tenochtitlán before it was conquered by Cortés? Here is an account of what a typical day for a male citizen in that city might have been like.

Compare Cultures

DIRECTIONS: Read the story about daily life in Tenochtitlán. Complete the table that follows to compare your daily life with that of an Aztec living in Tenochtitlán.

The merchant's guild has accepted me as a member. I am now ready to travel with a caravan of my own. How my life will change!

The temple trumpets guide the daily routine in Tenochtitlán. My stucco house has one bedroom for the whole family, one other small room, a bathroom, and no furniture except mats. At sunrise the sound of the temple trumpets wakes me and I bathe, put on my loin cloth, pick up food to eat later, and go to work. Before long I hear the trumpets again. Then I take the day's first meal and return to work. At about the time the sun is directly overhead, the trumpets signal me to return home to eat and to take a brief nap. After my nap, I go back to work until nightfall, when the trumpets sound the end of the workday.

At the end of the workday, I go home and spend time with my family until the trumpets blow again. Then I know it is time to go to sleep.

	YOU	AZTEC
Wake-Up Time		
Housing		
Meals		
Work		

22 ACTIVITY BOOK   Use after reading Chapter 4, Lesson 1, pages 149–153.

NAME _____ DATE _____

Estéban in Time and Place

Sequence Events

DIRECTIONS: Read the following quotations about Estéban, also known as Estevanico. Place the events discussed in the proper sequence by numbering the passages from 1 to 5, with 1 being the first event and 5 the last. Then use the information to answer the questions that follow.

____ "In 1538 Governor Mendoza organized an expedition to discover this land of great wealth and picked Father Marcos de Niza, a Franciscan friar, to lead it. Estevanico was his advance scout and advisor." *William Loren Katz*

____ "Estevanico traveled ahead of the main group, taking only a few Indians with him. The Indians could not speak Spanish, so Estevanico agreed to send Friar Marcos a cross made of twigs or tree branches to report his findings. A small cross would mean he had found nothing out of the ordinary. But if he found great cities he would send back a large cross." *Sibyl Hancock*

____ "Some historians, unfriendly toward the African, . . . [believe] he was murdered. One scholar believes Estevanico died for claiming to represent a powerful white country to Indians. Some historians have wondered if the young slave saw an opportunity for freedom and took it." *William Loren Katz*

____ "Not too much is known of his [Estéban's] early life. Born in Azamore, Morocco, around 1500, he was probably made captive as a teenager when Portugal's King Manoel seized the city in 1513." *William Loren Katz*

____ "[Estéban] . . . proceeded into the interior and sent back wooden crosses to indicate his progress. When his crosses increased in size until they were as tall as a man, the Spaniards realized that the [African] explorer had experienced great success. Indians brought news of Little Stephen's [Estéban's] approach to the fabulous seven cities about which so much had been heard." *John Hope Franklin*

1. In what country was Estéban born? _____

2. Who was chosen to lead the expedition? _____

3. List all of Estéban's jobs. _____

4. Reread Katz's different descriptions of Estéban's death. On a separate sheet of paper, write your own ending to the story of Estéban's search for the Seven Cities of Gold.

Use after reading Chapter 4, Lesson 2, pages 154–158.

Do You Speak *Spanish?*

Understand Word Origins

DIRECTIONS: Study the information in the dictionary box below. Use your textbook to help you fill in the blanks in the box. Then answer the questions that follow.

---

alligator came to English through Spanish. The Spanish word for "alligator" is *lagarto*. The Spanish word for "the" is *el*. When English speakers heard *el lagarto*, it sounded to them like "alligator."

armadillo a Spanish word meaning "armed man," or "little armored one." This word describes an animal whose body is almost entirely protected by an armorlike covering.

_____ comes from the Spanish word meaning "one who conquers by physical, mental, or moral force."

_____ a state name that comes from the Spanish word meaning "filled with flowers."

mosquito a Spanish and Portuguese word that means "little fly."

parakeet comes from the Spanish *periquito* and the Old French *paroquet*, both meaning "parrot."

---

1. What part of speech are all of these words? _____

2. Which word came to English through a misunderstanding? _____

3. Which words came to English from two different languages? _____

4. Which Spanish word is the name of a state? _____

5. On a separate sheet of paper, make a list of all the words you know that come from Spanish.

6. On the same sheet of paper, make a table with the following headings: ANIMALS, PEOPLE, PLACES. Write the words from the dictionary box and the words from the list you made for question 5 under the proper headings. Circle the category heading under which you have the most words.

NAME _____ DATE _____

HOW TO USE A MAP to Show Movement

Apply Map and Globe Skills

DIRECTIONS: Read the following paragraph and study the map. Then complete the activities below.

Potatoes were first grown by Inca Indians living in the Andes Mountains in northwestern South America. Spanish explorers in South America brought potatoes back to Spain. From Spain, potatoes were taken to Italy and England.

The English introduced the potato to Ireland and Scotland. Although English colonists brought potatoes to the colonies as early as 1621, potatoes did not become an important crop until the Irish immigrants brought them to New Hampshire in 1719.

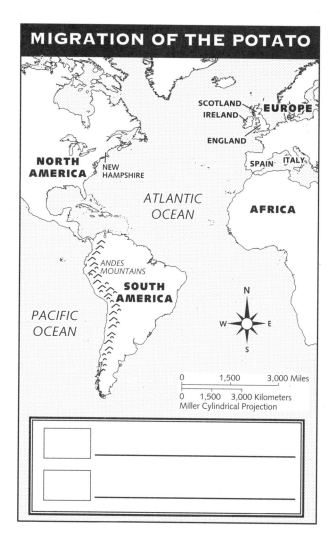

1. Imagine that you are a Spanish explorer. You have just set sail from an area near the Andes Mountains of South America. You are sailing south on the Pacific Ocean. Draw in red the route that you will follow to sail back to Spain.

2. Imagine that you are an Irish immigrant. You have just arrived in New Hampshire. Draw in blue the route that you followed as you sailed from Ireland to New Hampshire.

3. In the spaces provided, use the same two colors to make a map key to explain the information shown on your map.

Use after reading Chapter 4, Skill Lesson, pages 164–165.

NAME _____ DATE _____

Preparing Furs for Trade

The French bartered with the American Indians, exchanging European goods for beaver furs. At first the French did not hunt the beavers. American Indians trapped the beavers and prepared the beaver skins, or pelts, for trade.

Read a Flow Chart

DIRECTIONS: Study the flow chart that shows the steps American Indians followed to tan and cure beaver skins. Then answer the questions that follow.

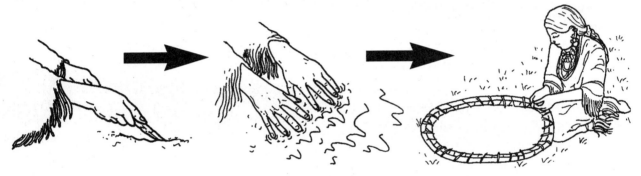

Step 1
Scraping: Scraping the pelt with a stick to clean it

Step 2
Tanning: Rubbing the pelt with marrow (sticky center of bone)

Step 3
Curing: Drying the scraped and tanned pelt on a stretching frame

1. What was the first step in preparing the beaver skins for trade? _____

2. Describe the tanning process. _____

3. What was the final step in preparing the hide for trade? _____

4. Rewrite these steps in the correct order: tanning, scraping, curing.

_____

NAME _____ DATE _____

HARVEST FESTIVALS

Was the Pilgrims' Thanksgiving the first Thanksgiving? You already know that there are many ideas about the first Thanksgiving in the Americas. What about the rest of the world? People around the world have held harvest festivals since they first harvested crops.

Compare Holiday Celebrations

DIRECTIONS: Study the chart below to learn about harvest festivals around the world. Next, complete the chart by filling in the information for the United States. Then use the chart to complete the activities that follow.

HARVEST FESTIVALS

PLACE	NAME OF FESTIVAL	WHEN HELD	FESTIVITIES
India	In honor of Gauri, goddess of the harvest and women	September	Offerings of milk and sweets to Gauri; feasting
Israel	Sukkot (also called the Feast of Tabernacles)	Autumn	Special shelters called succahs or tabernacles are built
Ancient China	Hhung-Ch'iu (the birthday of the moon)	Fifteenth day of the eighth month	Round moon cakes and round fruits on altars
England	Harvest Home	Harvest time; autumn	Feasting on roast beef, pudding; songs
Inca Empire	The Song of the Harvest	May (autumn in Southern Hemisphere)	Offering of first corn to their gods
United States			

1. During which season of the year are most harvest festivals held?

_____

2. Why do you think the Incas celebrated their harvest festival in May?

_____

_____

3. On a separate sheet of paper, describe what you think would be the perfect Thanksgiving Day celebration, from the beginning of the day to the end.

Use after reading Chapter 4, Lesson 5, pages 171–177.

NAME _____ DATE _____

HOW TO READ Parallel Time Lines

Apply Chart and Graph Skills

DIRECTIONS: *The parallel time lines below list events that happened in many different places. Study the time lines and then answer the questions that follow.*

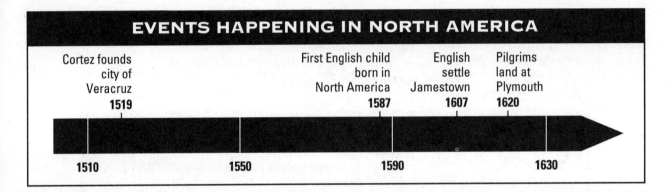

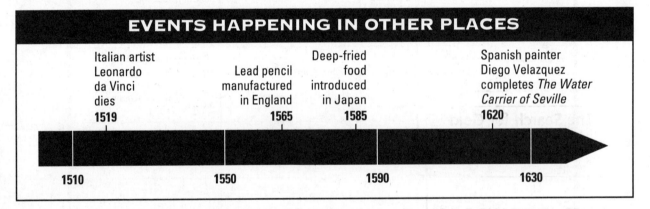

1. In which year did the English settle Jamestown? _____

2. Which event occurred first—Diego Velazquez's completion of *The Water Carrier of Seville* or Leonardo da Vinci's death? _____

3. Was the first lead pencil manufactured in England before or after the first English child was born in North America? _____

4. What was happening in North America in the same year that Diego Velazquez completed *The Water Carrier of Seville*? _____

NAME _____ DATE _____

Encounters in the Americas

Connect Main Ideas

DIRECTIONS: Use this organizer to show how the chapter's main ideas are connected. Write the main idea of each lesson.

Conquest of the Aztecs and Incas

The English in the Americas

Encounters in the Americas

The Search for Gold and Riches

New People in America

Encounters with the French and Dutch

Use after reading Chapter 4, pages 148–181.

NAME _____ DATE _____

Comparing Spanish Missions

The mission of San Antonio de Valero was built by the Catholic Church in what is now Texas. This mission was later given a new name—Pueblo del Alamo, later known as the Alamo.

Understand Diagrams

DIRECTIONS: *Compare the diagram below with the diagram of a Spanish mission shown on pages 198–199 in your textbook. Write an* **S** *next to each statement that describes a Spanish mission. Write an* **A** *next to each statement that describes the Alamo. Write* **SA** *next to each statement that describes both missions.*

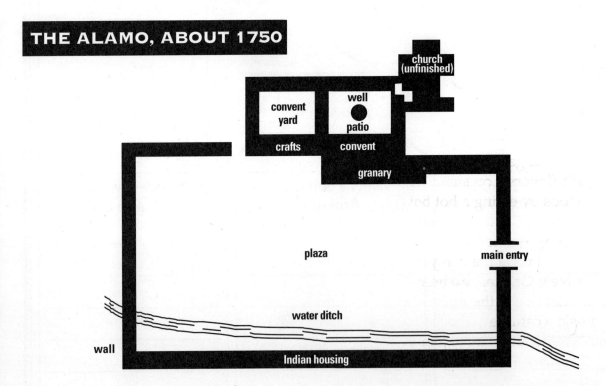

____ water source outside mission   ____ missionaries housed inside mission

____ all crafts contained within mission walls   ____ ranch workers housed outside mission

____ large, open area in center of mission   ____ walls surround entire mission

____ mission includes a church   ____ patio within mission walls

30 ACTIVITY BOOK   Use after reading Chapter 5, Lesson 1, pages 195–200.

NAME _____ DATE _____

Europeans Settle Throughout
NORTH AMERICA

Connect Main Ideas

DIRECTIONS: Use this organizer to show how the chapter's main ideas are connected. Write three examples to support each main idea.

The Spanish Borderlands
The Spanish government decided to expand its land in North America.

1. _____
2. _____
3. _____

The Growth of New France
The French government took steps to protect its interests in New France.

1. _____
2. _____
3. _____

Europeans Settle Throughout North America

The New England Colonies
The New England colonists set up different colonies.

1. _____
2. _____
3. _____

The Middle Colonies
People from different cultures contributed to life in the middle colonies.

1. _____
2. _____
3. _____

The Southern Colonies
Selling crops was important to the people in the southern colonies.

1. _____
2. _____
3. _____

Use after reading Chapter 5, pages 194–227.

NAME _____ DATE _____

Having a WHALE of a Time

New London, Connecticut; New Bedford, Massachusetts; and Sag Harbor, New York, were once important whaling centers. By the 1970s whalers had killed so many whales that many species were near extinction. In 1972 the United States Marine Mammal Protection Act stopped the widespread slaughter of whales by United States citizens. Many other countries have passed similar laws.

Link History to Science

DIRECTIONS: Use the information above and the diagram below to complete the activities following the diagram.

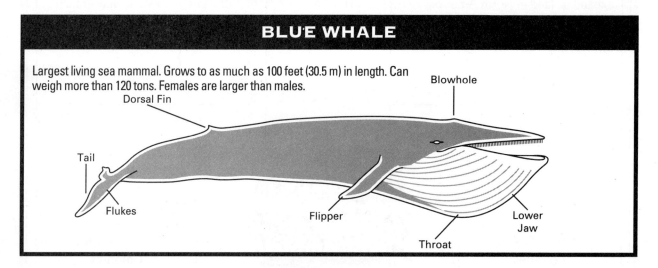

1. Whales are mammals that need to breathe air into their lungs. They must come to the surface of the water every few minutes to breathe. Whales' nostrils are in the top of their heads. Put an **X** over the part of the whale where you would find its nostrils.

2. The blue whale travels at speeds up to $15^{1}/_{2}$ miles per hour. Circle each part of the whale that helps it balance and steer through the water.

3. The blue whale has grooves on its throat that help it trap mouthfuls of "sea soup." Shade or color this part of the whale.

4. Why was the Marine Mammal Protection Act passed? _____

_____

5. On a separate sheet of paper, write a paragraph explaining why you do or do not think it is important to pass laws that protect whales from hunters.

NAME _____ DATE _____

HOW TO READ a Circle Graph

Apply Chart and Graph Skills

DIRECTIONS: *The circle graph below shows how the population of New York State was divided in 1800. Study the graph and then answer the questions that follow.*

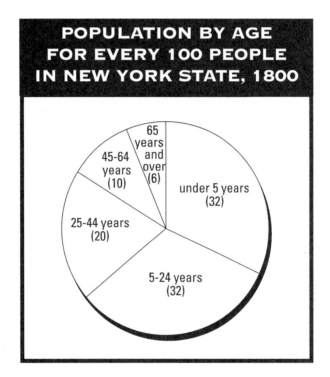

1. In 1800, for every 100 people in New York State, how many were between the ages of 25 and 44? _____

2. What was the smallest age group in New York State? _____

3. Which were the largest age groups in New York State in 1800? _____
_____

4. For every 100 people, which was larger: the age group 25–44 years or the combined age groups of 45–64 years and 65 years and over? _____

5. For every 100 people, was the population of those aged 24 years and younger more than or less than half of the overall population of New York State in 1800? _____
_____

Use after reading Chapter 6, Skill Lesson, page 234.

NAME _____ DATE _____

Looking at Life in the Southern Colonies

Do you think you would be ready at age 17 to take over the business of three plantations? Eliza Lucas did just that. She did not have a choice. The Lucas family moved from the West Indies to South Carolina when Eliza was 16 years old. Soon after her father went off to fight a war, her mother fell seriously ill and Eliza was left in charge.

Describe Life on a Plantation

DIRECTIONS: Study Eliza Lucas's own words. Try to understand her daily life. Then write E next to each statement that describes Eliza's life.

After being left in charge of the plantations, Eliza wrote the following to a friend in England:

> "I have the business of three plantations to transact . . . [which] requires much writing and more business and fatigue of other sorts than you can imagine."

After experiencing what it was like to run the three plantations, Eliza wrote of her daily routine:

> "I rise at five o'clock in the morning, read till seven, then take a walk in the garden or fields, see that the servants are at their respective business. . . . The first hour after breakfast is spent at music, the next is constantly employed in recollecting something I have learned, such as French or shorthand."

_____ 1. I am tired from all the writing and business that is part of managing three plantations.

_____ 2. I have basically the same daily routine as other teenagers.

_____ 3. I spend much of the early morning reading.

_____ 4. It is important to remember what you read and learn.

_____ 5. No teenager is able to take charge of a business.

_____ 6. I spend my whole day working and have no time for fun.

_____ 7. It is important to be up before sunrise.

_____ 8. Taking a walk in the garden or fields is a waste of time.

DIRECTIONS: On a separate sheet of paper, write a brief description of your daily routine. How does your daily routine compare to Eliza Lucas's? Do you see life the same way?

NAME _____ DATE _____

TOOLING Around the Frontier

Sequence with Visuals

DIRECTIONS: *The diagram below shows how the broadax was used to make lumber to build cabins. Study the diagram. Then place the steps on the right in the proper sequence by numbering them from 1 through 10.*

USING THE BROADAX TO MAKE LUMBER

Step 1 Making chalk line on bark-stripped log. Four chalk lines are made by "twanging" a chalked cord onto log to square off log.

Chalk Line

_____ Strip bark.

_____ Snap chalk lines.

_____ Hew log to chalk lines.

_____ Stand on log and hold felling ax.

_____ Fell, or cut down, tree.

_____ Stand next to log and hold broadax.

_____ Place "dog" to hold log.

_____ Make vertical cuts in log.

_____ Place chalk lines on log.

_____ Notch ends of log to use to build cabin.

Step 2 Scoring to chalk line. Stand on log and hold long-handled felling ax. Use felling ax to make deep vertical cuts up to chalk line. This is known as "scoring."

Felling Ax | Dog

Step 3 Hewing to chalk line. Stand alongside log. Hold broadax with two hands. Place one knee next to log. Use broadax to hew, or split off, the vertical cuts made in Step 2.

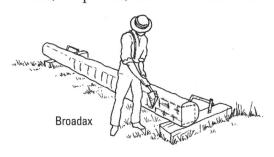
Broadax

Use after reading Chapter 6, Lesson 3, pages 241–245.

ACTIVITY BOOK 41

NAME _____ DATE _____

HOW TO USE a Product Map
to Make Generalizations

Apply Map and Globe Skills

DIRECTIONS: Use the map below to complete the following activities.

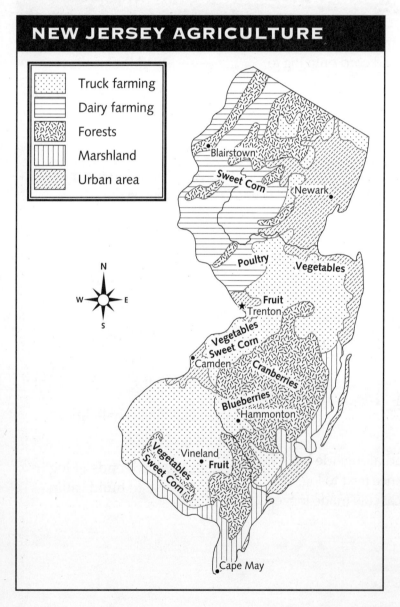

NEW JERSEY AGRICULTURE

Legend:
- Truck farming
- Dairy farming
- Forests
- Marshland
- Urban area

1. Draw a line from Newark to Cape May. Identify the different areas you would pass through if you traveled from north to south along this line.

   _____

   _____

2. What city in New Jersey is located in the area where cranberries and blueberries are grown?

   _____

3. What is the main use of land around Vineland?

   _____

4. What crop grows in most parts of New Jersey?

   _____

5. Would you be more likely to be a farmer if you lived in Vineland, Cape May, or Newark?

   _____

42 ACTIVITY BOOK   Use after reading Chapter 6, Skill Lesson, pages 246–247.

NAME _____ DATE _____

LIFE IN THE BRITISH COLONIES

Connect Main Ideas

DIRECTIONS: Use this organizer to compare the ways of life of early colonists. Write three examples for each place.

Life in the British Colonies

Life in Towns and Cities
1. _____
2. _____
3. _____

Life on Plantations
1. _____
2. _____
3. _____

Life on the Frontier
1. _____
2. _____
3. _____

Use after reading Chapter 6, pages 228–249.

NAME _____ DATE _____

HISTORICAL EVENTS OF THE 1700s

Apply Chart and Graph Skills

DIRECTIONS: Write the number of each event at the correct place on the time line. Be sure to place the number of the event at the correct date and on the correct side of the time line.

1. **1755** Earthquake shocks Lisbon, Portugal, killing at least 10,000 people
2. **1747** Virginia settlers and Pennsylvania traders move into Ohio Territory
3. **1760** Daniel Boone hired to scout the frontier in present-day eastern Tennessee
4. **1755** British drive French settlers out of Acadia
5. **1749** Philadelphia founds what becomes the University of Pennsylvania
6. **1726** Jonathan Swift's novel, *Gulliver's Travels*, is an instant success in Europe
7. **1750** Johann Sebastian Bach, the great composer, dies in Germany
8. **1763** Proclamation of 1763 bans settlement west of the Appalachian Mountains
9. **1753** French in Canada move into British lands in Ohio River valley
10. **1718** Pirate known as Blackbeard killed in sea battle off North Carolina coast
11. **1759** British win Battle of Quebec, capturing city
12. **1754** Opening battle of French and Indian War
13. **1763** The French and Indian War ends
14. **1756** British declare war on French in Europe, starting the Seven Years' War

44 ACTIVITY BOOK

NAME _____ DATE _____

HOW TO USE A Historical Map

Apply Map and Globe Skills

DIRECTIONS:
The map on this page shows where some large immigrant groups were concentrated during the colonial period. Study the map. Then answer the questions that follow.

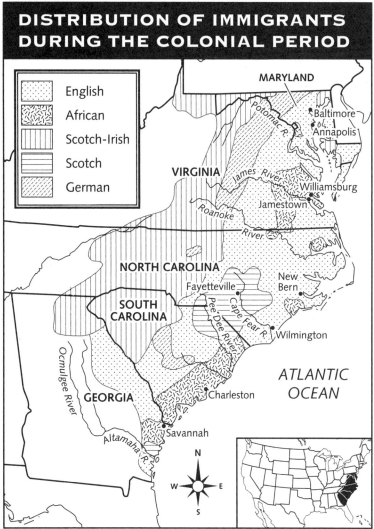

1. Which immigrant group settled farthest west? _____

2. Which immigrant group settled farthest south? _____

3. Where did most of the Africans settle? _____
_____

4. Which immigrant groups settled in all of the southern colonies?
_____

Use after reading Chapter 7, Skill Lesson, pages 268–269.

ACTIVITY BOOK 45

UNDERSTANDING PROVERBS IN *Poor Richard's Almanack*

Benjamin Franklin, a respected colonist, was and still is known for his political and scientific work. He was also a writer and printer who published a yearly almanac called *Poor Richard's Almanack*. Franklin's yearly almanacs were popular with the colonists because they contained a variety of features, including calendars, weather predictions, and recipes.

Analyze the Meaning of Proverbs

DIRECTIONS: Franklin also included proverbs in his almanac. A proverb is a short, commonly used saying that expresses a general truth. Below are some proverbs from Poor Richard's Almanack. Circle the statement below each proverb that best describes what the proverb means.

1. **Early to bed and early to rise makes a man healthy, wealthy, and wise.**

   You will benefit from good habits and hard work.

   You will be rich if you stick to your bedtime.

2. **Sell not virtue to purchase wealth, nor liberty to purchase power.**

   You will lose money if you try to buy wealth or power.

   Do not sacrifice your values for money or power.

3. **Don't throw stones at your neighbors, if your own windows are glass.**

   Do not criticize others, because you have faults, too.

   You can do what you want to others if you protect yourself first.

4. **Make haste slowly.**

   Consider your actions carefully.

   If you hurry, you can get more done.

5. **Tart words make no friends: a spoonful of honey will catch more flies than a gallon of vinegar.**

   Speak kindly to others and you will have many friends.

   You will make many friends if you feed them honey.

6. **Never leave that till tomorrow which you can do today.**

   Get your work done today so you will not have more work tomorrow.

   It's always better to leave work for the next day.

7. **No gains without pains.**

   Life is hard.

   To get better at something, you must work hard at it.

8. **Being ignorant is not so much a shame as being unwilling to learn.**

   It is a waste not to be eager for an education.

   People who are not smart are sad.

NAME _____ DATE _____

Events Leading to Revolution

Colonial printers turned out news sheets that often were hung in public places. These sheets told of events happening in the colonies.

Write Historical News Stories

DIRECTIONS: Imagine you are writing a news sheet in the colonies. For each date below, write a headline for and a description of an important historical event.

December 1773

_____
_____
_____
_____
_____
_____

April 18, 1775

_____
_____
_____
_____
_____
_____

September 1774

_____
_____
_____
_____
_____
_____

April 19, 1775

_____
_____
_____
_____
_____
_____

Use after reading Chapter 7, Lesson 3, pages 279–284.

NAME _____ DATE _____

HOW TO MAKE Economic Choices

Apply Critical Thinking Skills

DIRECTIONS: Imagine you have $20 to spend. Then complete the graphic organizer that follows to help you make an economic choice.

CHOICES
List three $20 items you would like to buy.

OPPORTUNITY COSTS
List the value each item has to you.

ECONOMIC CHOICE
Compare the value of what you will be giving up, or the opportunity costs, for each choice. What are you willing to give up, or trade off? Make an economic choice based on which item will best meet your needs with the $20 you have to spend. List that item below. Your other choices become your trade-offs.

Use after reading Chapter 7, Skill Lesson, page 285.

NAME _____ DATE _____

DIFFERENCES DIVIDE
Britain and Its Colonies

Connect Main Ideas

DIRECTIONS: Use this organizer to show how the chapter's main ideas are connected. Write three details to support each main idea.

Britain Rules the Colonies → **Differences Divide Britain and Its Colonies** → **Britain and the Colonies Go to War**

Government in the Colonies
The British colonists became unhappy with British rule.

1. _____
2. _____
3. _____

Quarrels and Conflicts
Individuals and groups in the British colonies worked to make changes in their government.

1. _____
2. _____
3. _____

Colonists Unite
The colonists came together as they protested British rule.

1. _____
2. _____
3. _____

Use after reading Chapter 7, pages 262–287.

ACTIVITY BOOK 49

The Redcoats ARE COMING!

Compare Visuals

DIRECTIONS: Compare the drawings of the Continental soldier's uniform and the British soldier's uniform. Then write C next to each statement below that describes a Continental uniform. Write B next to each statement that describes a British uniform. Write CB next to each statement that describes both uniforms.

Continental Uniform

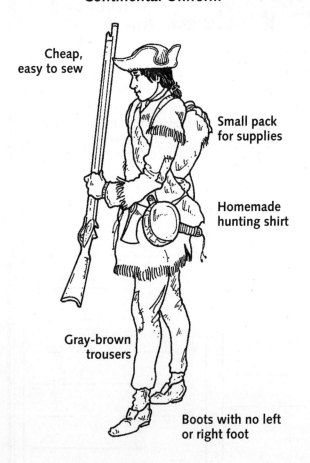

- Cheap, easy to sew
- Small pack for supplies
- Homemade hunting shirt
- Gray-brown trousers
- Boots with no left or right foot

British Uniform

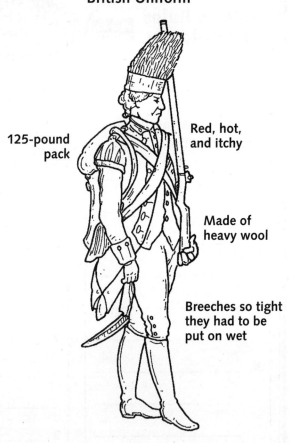

- 125-pound pack
- Red, hot, and itchy
- Made of heavy wool
- Breeches so tight they had to be put on wet

_____ hotter uniform

_____ more visible in woods

_____ included a musket

_____ included a pack

_____ more practical

_____ included a canteen

_____ knee-length boots

_____ fringed shirt

_____ three-cornered hat

_____ included an ax

NAME _____   DATE _____

HOW TO READ a Political Cartoon

Apply Reading and Research Skills

DIRECTIONS: France was an ally of the colonists during the American Revolution. Examine the political cartoon below. Then answer the questions that follow.

NOVEMBER 1780
French General, Count De Rochambeau, Reviewing the French Troops in America

1. When was this political cartoon drawn? _____

2. What conclusions can you draw about the cartoonist's opinion of the French soldiers?
_____

3. What specific items in the cartoon led you to your conclusion?
_____
_____

Use after reading Chapter 8, Skill Lesson, page 294.

NAME _____ DATE _____

A Woman Printed the Declaration of Independence

Only men drafted and signed the Declaration of Independence. Read the passage below to find out why Mary Katharine Goddard was chosen to print the Declaration of Independence.

Read Line by Line for Comprehension

DIRECTIONS: Use the line numbers in the passage to help you answer the questions that follow.

1   The Declaration of Independence was signed on July 4, 1776. By January 1777, it had
2   been printed seven times! There was, however, no official copy of the Declaration.
3   So, on January 18, 1777, Congress decided to print official copies for each state in
4   the new union.
5   The members of Congress wanted to find a local printer. This meant that they would
6   look in Baltimore, because that was where they were meeting. (By then, the British had
7   taken Philadelphia.) The logical choice was Mary Katharine Goddard.
8   Goddard was well known and experienced. She had a reputation for being a high-
9   quality printer. Goddard had learned the printing trade from her brother. She printed
10 her own newspaper, the *Maryland Journal,* and had even been the head of the post office of
11 Baltimore since 1775!
12 How can you tell the difference between the Declaration that Goddard printed and the other
13 copies? The one Goddard printed lists the delegates' names in neat columns next to the
14 states they represented. On the very bottom of the document, you will find "Baltimore,
15 In Maryland: Printed by Mary Katharine Goddard."

1. Which line tells you the number of times the Declaration had been printed by January 1777? _____

2. Which lines tell that Congress wanted to print official copies? _____

3. Lines 5–7 tell why the members of Congress wanted to find a printer in Baltimore. What was their reason? _____

4. Reread lines 8–11. List the reasons Congress chose Goddard as the printer.

_____

5. List the line numbers of the paragraph that explains how to tell the difference between the Declaration that Goddard printed and the other copies. _____

NAME _____ DATE _____

HOW TO LEARN FROM PICTURES

Apply Critical Thinking Skills

DIRECTIONS: By studying a picture carefully, you can learn a variety of information about a subject. Study the picture below of Patrick Henry speaking to The House of Burgesses against the Stamp Act. Then answer the questions that follow.

1. What part of the picture did you look at first? Why?

_____

_____

_____

2. Are the people who are listening to Patrick Henry interested in what he is saying? How can you tell?

_____

_____

_____

3. How do you think the people in the picture feel? How can you tell?

_____

_____

_____

Use after reading Chapter 8, Skill Lesson, page 300.

AMERICANS TAKE SIDES

Not all of the people living in the British colonies supported the fight for independence from Britain. About one third sided with the Loyalists, another third sided with the Patriots, and another third remained neutral.

Categorize Information

DIRECTIONS: Write the following names or groups of people in the appropriate category in the chart below. You may wish to reread pages 301–305 in your textbook.

Abigail Adams
John Adams
General Thomas Gage
Patrick Henry
Richard Henry Lee
Peter Muhlenberg
John Murray
Thomas Paine
Peter Salem
Mary Slocumb
Ethiopian Regiment
most Native Americans
many northern Anglicans
many southern Presbyterians
Quakers
Unmarried Ladies of America

LOYALIST	PATRIOT	NEUTRAL

NAME _____ DATE _____

Characterize Patriots

Map Characters in a Story

DIRECTIONS: Use the characters in Samuel's Choice to complete the organizer below. Describe each character's role by filling in the appropriate box.

SAMUEL ABRAHAM	SANA

THOMAS JEFFERSON	ISAAC VAN DITMAS

SAMUEL'S CHOICE

TOBY AND NATHANIEL	MORDECAI GIST	GEORGE WASHINGTON

Use after reading Chapter 8, Lesson 4, pages 306–309.

Which Event Happened First?

Sequence Events

DIRECTIONS: In each pair of events of the American Revolution, circle the event that happened first.

1.	Committees of Correspondence formed	Second Continental Congress formed
2.	Second Continental Congress formed	Battle of Lexington and Concord
3.	Second Continental Congress formed	Olive Branch Petition sent to King George III
4.	Winter at Valley Forge	Battle of Bunker Hill
5.	Richard Henry Lee gives speech to Second Continental Congress declaring free and independent states	Thomas Paine's *Common Sense* published
6.	Jefferson plans the Declaration	Second Continental Congress formed
7.	George Washington's troops almost wiped out after winter at Valley Forge	Declaration of Independence signed
8.	Colonists' victory at Saratoga	French join Revolution on colonists' side
9.	Treaty of Paris signed in 1783	Battle of Yorktown
10.	Treaty of Paris signed in 1783	Benedict Arnold becomes a traitor

NAME _____ DATE _____

The War for Independence

Connect Main Ideas

DIRECTIONS: Use this organizer to show how the chapter's main ideas are connected. Write the main idea of each lesson.

The War for Independence

- At War with the Homeland → _____
- The Decision for Independence → _____
- Americans Take Sides → _____
- Victory and Independence → _____

Use after reading Chapter 8, pages 288–319.

NAME _____ DATE _____

Articles of Confederation

The Articles of Confederation united 13 independent states. The Articles gave the national government certain powers, but because Americans wanted to guard their newly won freedom, the national government they formed was weak.

Identify Reasons

DIRECTIONS: Study the table below. It lists weaknesses of the Articles of Confederation. Complete the table by filling in a reason for each weakness.

WEAKNESS	REASON
There was no strong national government.	
At least 9 of the 13 states had to agree on any law or decision.	
No single leader controlled the government.	
Congress could not raise a national army without the permission of the states.	
Congress could not collect taxes.	
Congress could not make laws about trade.	

Who Was There?

Identify Historical Figures

DIRECTIONS: From the list at the right, choose the person who might be describing his part in the Constitutional Convention. Write the letter identifying his name in the correct blank below.

A. John Adams
B. Patrick Henry
C. John Hancock
D. Thomas Jefferson
E. Daniel Shays
F. Benjamin Franklin
G. James Madison
H. Gouverneur Morris
I. George Washington
J. Samuel Adams

_____ 1. In 1779 I was elected to represent Virginia as a member of Congress under the Articles of Confederation.

_____ 2. I was elected president of the Constitutional Convention.

_____ 3. I was sick, so I could not attend the Constitutional Convention.

_____ 4. I refused to take part in the Constitutional Convention because I did not believe that a stronger national government was a good idea.

_____ 5. I said of the Constitutional Convention, "It really is an assembly of demigods."

_____ 6. I was Congress's youngest member at 29 years of age.

_____ 7. I was carried to the Constitutional Convention in a Chinese sedan chair.

_____ 8. I could not attend the Constitutional Convention because I was in Paris as the United States ambassador to France.

_____ 9. I changed the opening words in the Preamble to the Constitution to read, "We the people of the United States. . . ."

_____ 10. I could not attend the Constitutional Convention because I was in London as the United States ambassador to Britain.

_____ 11. I was too busy as governor of Massachusetts to attend the convention.

_____ 12. As a frontier farmer, I was not invited to the convention.

_____ 13. I was given the job of writing down all the ideas that were approved during the convention.

_____ 14. I was the most honored hero of the American Revolution.

NAME _____   DATE _____

HOW TO FIGURE TRAVEL TIME AND DISTANCE

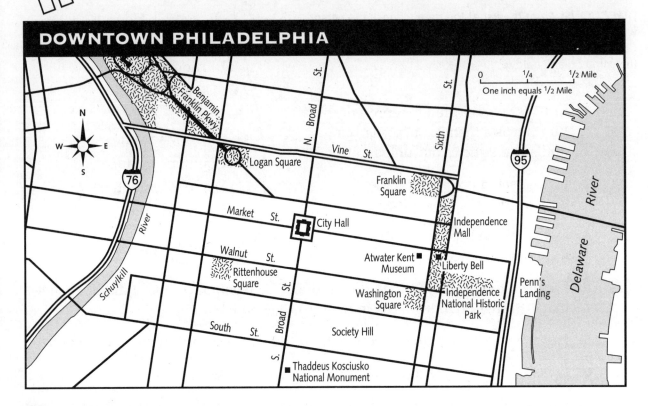

 Apply Map and Globe Skills

DIRECTIONS: Study the map above to complete the following activities.

1. Draw the following route on the map: You are at the Liberty Bell. Go west on Market Street to City Hall. Head south on S. Broad Street to Thaddeus Kosciusko National Monument.

2. On this map, 1 inch stands for ½ mile. Use a ruler to measure the number of inches covered by the route you drew. Write your answer here. _____

3. Multiply the total number of inches traveled by ½ (the number of miles equal to 1 inch). This will tell you the total number of miles that would be traveled if you walked this route in Philadelphia. _____

4. To find out how long it would take to travel this route at different speeds, divide the total number of miles by the rate of travel shown below.

   Walking (3 mph): _____

   Jogging (6 mph): _____

60 ACTIVITY BOOK   Use after reading Chapter 9, Skill Lesson, pages 344–345.

NAME _____ DATE _____

Who Has the Power?

Compare Government Systems

DIRECTIONS: Use the diagram on page 347 of your textbook and the information from Chapter 9 to complete the following activities. Put an N next to powers that belong to the national government, an S next to powers that belong to state governments, and a B next to powers that are shared by both.

_____ 1. Raise money by taxing citizens

_____ 2. Set up public schools

_____ 3. Set rules for state and local elections

_____ 4. Print and coin money

_____ 5. Raise an army and a navy

_____ 6. Make laws for immigration

_____ 7. Control trade among states

_____ 8. Control trade within states

_____ 9. Set up courts

_____ 10. Declare war

_____ 11. Admit new states

_____ 12. Make laws for marriage and divorce

DIRECTIONS: Compare the powers granted to the national government by the Constitution with those granted to it by the Articles of Confederation. Use the information above to complete the activities that follow. You may need to review Lesson 1 on the Articles of Confederation.

1. Put a check mark next to those powers of the national government that are the same under the Constitution as they were under the Articles of Confederation.

2. Circle the powers of the national government that are new under the Constitution.

3. Think about what your life might be like if the Articles of Confederation still governed the United States. Then use information summarized in the activities on this page to write a paragraph that explains why the Constitution made the United States a stronger country.

_____

_____

_____

_____

_____

NAME _____ DATE _____

HOW TO COMPROMISE TO RESOLVE CONFLICTS

Apply Participation Skills

DIRECTIONS: Complete the graphic organizer that follows. For each step, write in the arguments, decisions, or both made at the Constitutional Convention that led to the Great Compromise.

BOTH SIDES CLEARLY STATE WANTS AND NEEDS

↓

BOTH SIDES UNDERSTAND WHAT IS TO BE GIVEN UP

↓

BOTH SIDES DECIDE WHAT IS MOST IMPORTANT

↓

BOTH SIDES DISCUSS POSSIBLE COMPROMISES

↓

BOTH SIDES VOTE ON COMPROMISES

NAME _____ DATE _____

Who Does What in THE GOVERNMENT?

Diagram the United States Government

DIRECTIONS: Study the diagram on page 354 of your textbook that shows how a bill becomes a law. Then order the steps of the process below from 1 to 6.

____ The bill becomes a law or is sent back to Congress for another vote.

____ A member of the House or the Senate introduces a bill.

____ The President reviews the bill.

____ Congressional committees review the bill.

____ The President either vetoes the bill or signs it into law.

____ Both houses of Congress vote to approve the bill.

DIRECTIONS: Study the diagram on page 356 of your textbook that shows how checks and balances work. Then complete the chart below by writing in the branch that holds each particular power and the branch being checked. The first one has been completed for you.

BRANCH HOLDING AUTHORITY	CHECK/BALANCE	BRANCH BEING CHECKED
Legislative	Override the President's veto	Executive
	Appoint Supreme Court justices	
	Rule President's actions unconstitutional	
	Veto a bill	
	Approve treaties	
	Approve appointments of Supreme Court justices	

Use after reading Chapter 9, Lesson 4, pages 353–357.

NAME _____ DATE _____

Constitutional Footnotes

Understand a Primary Source

DIRECTIONS: Read the Preamble to the United States Constitution below. Then figure out what the footnoted, or numbered, words and phrases mean. Write the number of the footnote next to the best explanation.

> We the people of the United States,
>   in order to form a more perfect Union,[1]
>   establish justice,[2]
>   insure domestic tranquillity,[3]
>   provide for the common defense,[4]
>   promote the general welfare,[5] and
>   secure the blessings of liberty[6]
>   to ourselves[7]
>   and our posterity,[8]
>   do ordain[9]
>   and establish[10]
>   this Constitution for the United States of America.

_____ **a.** set up a fair system

_____ **b.** set up

_____ **c.** make sure there is peace at home

_____ **d.** make a better government

_____ **e.** make official

_____ **f.** supply protection for all

_____ **g.** encourage health, happiness, and comfort

_____ **h.** gain and keep the gifts of freedom

_____ **i.** everyone who later becomes part of this country

_____ **j.** everyone belonging to this country

NAME _____ DATE _____

The Constitution

Connect Main Ideas

DIRECTIONS: Use this organizer to show how the chapter's main ideas are connected. Write the main idea of each lesson, and list the three branches of government.

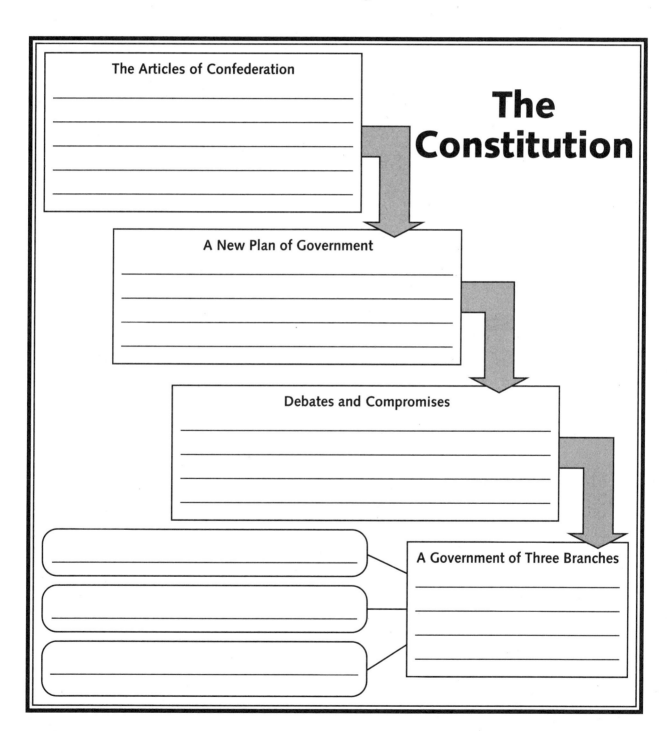

Use after reading Chapter 9, pages 332–365.

ACTIVITY BOOK 65

NAME _____ DATE _____

The MAZE of RATIFICATION

Sequence States

DIRECTIONS: Use the map and the table on page 369 of your textbook to get through the maze of ratification. Draw a line from Start to the first state to ratify the Constitution. Then continue through the maze to connect the remaining states in the order of their ratification.

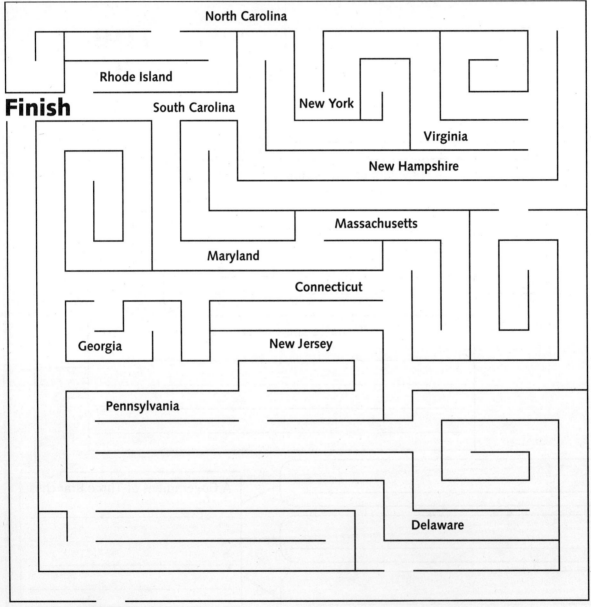

66 ACTIVITY BOOK

NAME _____ DATE _____

Counting the Amendments

Number the Bill of Rights

DIRECTIONS: Read the list of freedoms below, and decide which amendment protects each one. Write the amendment's number in the box opposite each freedom. If all your answers are correct, you can add the numbers in each of the three columns and one of your totals will equal the number of amendments in the Bill of Rights. Circle the correct total.

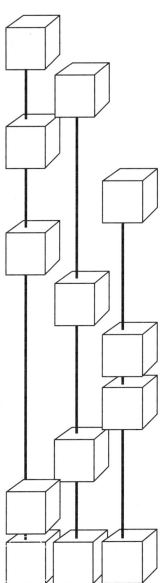

1. Right to "keep and bear arms"

2. Right to a speedy and public trial

3. Freedom of speech

4. Freedom to hold meetings and to ask the government to hear complaints

5. Freedom from being forced to quarter soldiers

6. Protection of rights that are not listed in the Constitution

7. Freedom of religion

8. Protection against the national government's doing things not listed in the Constitution

9. Freedom of the press

10. Protection against the government's ordering an unreasonable search of a home

TOTAL NUMBER OF AMENDMENTS IN BILL OF RIGHTS

Use after reading Chapter 10, Lesson 2, pages 374–377.

NAME ______________________________ DATE ______________

Who's in Office?

Organize Information

DIRECTIONS: Complete the following graphic organizer about the first United States government under the Constitution. Use the information in your textbook as a guide.

THE FIRST U.S. GOVERNMENT

EXECUTIVE BRANCH

President

____

Vice President

____

CABINET

Secretary of ____________________ was ____________________

Secretary of ____________________ was ____________________

Secretary of ____________________ was ____________________

Attorney ____________________ was ____________________

LEGISLATIVE BRANCH

The two houses

____

____

JUDICIAL BRANCH

Chief Justice

____

Use after reading Chapter 10, Lesson 3, pages 378–384.

NAME _____ DATE _____

HOW TO LEARN FROM A DOCUMENT

This résumé, or summary of experience, lists information Benjamin Banneker might have written about himself. The cover of Banneker's almanac lists information about his publication.

Résumé
BENJAMIN BANNEKER

- Born in Baltimore, Maryland, 1731
- Son of free Africans
- Learned to read from grandmother
- Self-taught in mathematics and astronomy
- Talented in mechanical sciences
- Made first wooden clock in America
- First important African scientist in the United States
- Served for two years on the commission to survey and plan the city of Washington, D.C.
- Wrote and published annual almanac with at least 29 editions

Apply Reading and Research Skills

DIRECTIONS: Study the two documents above. Then complete the activities that follow.

1. Underline the title of Banneker's publication.

2. Circle the year in which Banneker's work was published.

3. Put a star next to the city in which Banneker's work was printed.

4. What do you think is Banneker's most interesting accomplishment? Explain why.

_____

_____

Use after reading Chapter 10, Skill Lesson, page 385.

NAME _____ DATE _____

A New Government Begins

Connect Main Ideas

DIRECTIONS: Use this organizer to show how the chapter's main ideas are connected. Write a sentence or two describing how each idea shown below helped to build a new government.

A New Government Begins

Approving the Constitution

_____
_____
_____

Rights and Responsibilities

_____
_____
_____

Putting the New Government to Work

_____
_____
_____

BLAZING A TRAIL WEST

Identify Historical Figures

DIRECTIONS: On the blanks provided, write the word or name that best completes each sentence. Some letters in your answers will have numbers under them. Write these letters in the appropriate boxes below, and you will find the name of Daniel Boone's wife.

1. After the Revolutionary War, the land between the Appalachian Mountains and the Mississippi River was called the American ___ ___ ___ ___ ___ ___ ___ ___.
                                                                                                                                1

2. Settlers west of the Appalachians were called ___ ___ ___ ___ ___ ___ ___ ___.
                                                              12

3. Daniel Boone came to love the woods and hunting after his family moved to the ___ ___ ___ ___ ___ ___   ___ ___ ___ ___ ___ ___ of North Carolina.
   10   11

4. A man named ___ ___ ___ ___   ___ ___ ___ ___ ___ ___ told Boone stories about land far to the west over the Appalachian Mountains.
                                                    4

5. After the French and Indian War, Boone set out to find an Indian trail called the ___ ___ ___ ___ ___ ___ ___ ' ___   ___ ___ ___ ___.
                                                                                              9

6. Boone told about the rich land and buffalo in ___ ___ ___ ___ ___ ___ ___ ___.
                                                                         6

7. Both the ___ ___ ___ ___ ___ ___ ___ ___ and Shawnees lived in settlements throughout Kentucky.
              5   2

8. Boone cleared a path through the Cumberland Gap that came to be known as the ___ ___ ___ ___ ___ ___ ___ ___ ___ ___   ___ ___ ___ ___.
                                                                                                                                       7

9. Boone built a fort in this wilderness and named the new pioneer settlement ___ ___ ___ ___ ___ ___ ___ ___ ___ ___ ___ ___.
   8   3

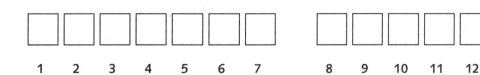

1	2	3	4	5	6	7	8	9	10	11	12

Use after reading Chapter 11, Lesson 1, pages 403–407.

NAME _____ DATE _____

Follow their Footsteps

Identify Historical Figures

DIRECTIONS: Each of the footprints below contains a paragraph that could have been written by one of the people involved with the Lewis and Clark expedition. Write the name of that person in the space provided.

One of my greatest accomplishments was the Louisiana Purchase. I asked the members of the Corps of Discovery to learn all they could about this new land.

_____

As chief of the Shoshones, I welcomed the members of the Corps of Discovery. I was especially happy to see my sister. To help Lewis and Clark make their way over the Rockies, I gave them horses.

_____

I was William Clark's slave. My skills in hunting and fishing made a valuable contribution to this exciting and informative expedition.

_____

The leader of the expedition was my good friend. He chose me to go on the expedition because of my skills in cartography. We called our group of explorers the Corps of Discovery.

_____

I was a Shoshone. The members of the expedition asked me to go with them to translate when they reached my tribe's lands. I agreed to go.

_____

After working as an army officer in the wilderness of the Northwest Territory, I led the expedition to explore the lands of the Louisiana Purchase. I kept a journal of our experiences.

_____

72 ACTIVITY BOOK   Use after reading Chapter 11, Lesson 2, pages 408–413.

NAME _____ DATE _____

The Growth of NATIONALISM

Understand Cause and Effect

DIRECTIONS: Complete the following chart. Fill in either the cause or the effect.

CAUSES	EFFECTS
_____ _____ _____	The Americans and the Indians fight in the Battle of Tippecanoe.
_____ _____ _____ _____ _____ _____ _____	War fever pushes Congress to declare war on Britain in 1812.
American Captain Oliver Hazard Perry defeats the British in a battle on Lake Erie on September 10, 1813.	_____ _____ _____
_____ _____	A wave of nationalism sweeps the country.
President Monroe wants to stop the growth of Spanish, French, and British colonies in the Americas.	_____ _____ _____

Use after reading Chapter 11, Lesson 3, pages 414–420.

ACTIVITY BOOK 73

NAME _____ DATE _____

HOW TO PREDICT A LIKELY OUTCOME

Apply Critical Thinking Skills

DIRECTIONS: The following flow chart lists the steps for predicting likely outcomes. Choose a school event, such as a test, that you expect to happen soon. Copy the flow chart onto another sheet of paper and use the steps to predict the outcome of the event.

- **THINK ABOUT WHAT YOU KNOW.**

- **MAKE A PREDICTION.**

- **READ OR GATHER MORE INFORMATION.**

- **ASK YOURSELF SOME QUESTIONS:**
  Does the new information support my prediction?
  Do I need to change my prediction?

- **DECIDE IF YOUR PREDICTION SEEMS CORRECT.**

- **GO THROUGH THE STEPS AGAIN, IF NECESSARY.**

Use after reading Chapter 11, Skill Lesson, page 421.

NAME _____ DATE _____

The Flag *was still there*

After the British attack on Fort McHenry, Francis Scott Key peered through the early dawn and saw that the American flag still flew over the fort. He wrote the words to "The Star-Spangled Banner," our national anthem, to honor this national symbol.

Understand Patriotic Symbols

DIRECTIONS: Read the statements below. Decide which statements tell how to respect and care for the flag and which statements give general information about the flag. Then place an X in the appropriate column.

THE FLAG	RESPECT/ CARE	GENERAL INFORMATION
1. The present flag has 64 separate elements.		
2. The flag has the exact shades of blue and red, which are numbers 70075 and 70180 in the *Standard Color Card of America*.		
3. The flag is to be flown at half-mast as a mark of respect after the death of a major official.		
4. The present flag dates back to July 4, 1960, when the fiftieth star was added for Hawaii.		
5. The flag is taken down in bad weather.		
6. The flag is never to be allowed to touch anything beneath it, such as the ground, the floor, or water.		
7. The United States flag is called the "Stars and Stripes."		
8. The flag that Key wrote about had 15 stars and 15 stripes.		
9. Congress passed a law in 1818 requiring the flag to have 13 stripes to represent the original 13 colonies.		
10. The flag is to be displayed during school days in or near every school.		

Use after reading Chapter 11, Lesson 4, pages 422–427.

NAME _____ DATE _____

ON THE MOVE

Connect Main Ideas

DIRECTIONS: Use this organizer to show how the chapter's main ideas are connected. Write one or two sentences to tell about each person or pair of people or to summarize each event or idea.

On the Move

Across the Appalachians

Daniel Boone _____
_____
_____
_____

Settling Kentucky _____
_____
_____
_____

Pioneer Life _____
_____
_____
_____

The Louisiana Purchase

The Purchase _____
_____
_____
_____

Lewis and Clark _____
_____
_____
_____

Zebulon Pike _____
_____
_____
_____

A Second War with Britain

Tecumseh and
the Prophet _____
_____
_____
_____

The War of 1812 _____
_____
_____
_____

The Era of Good Feelings __
_____
_____
_____

Use after reading Chapter 11, pages 402–429.

NAME _____ DATE _____

Inventors and their Inventions

Link Past Technology to the Present

DIRECTIONS: Complete the following chart about inventions of the Industrial Revolution by filling in the missing information.

INVENTOR	INVENTION	IMPORTANCE OF INVENTION	WHAT YOUR LIFE WOULD BE LIKE WITHOUT THE INVENTION
Unknown	spinning machine		
Eli Whitney			
	one-factory system		
		speeded travel and trade over water	
	locomotive, the *Tom Thumb*		

Use after reading Chapter 12, Lesson 1, pages 431–438.

NAME _____ DATE _____

The Trail of Tears

Sequence Events

DIRECTIONS: Read the following events leading up to the Trail of Tears. Then identify the year in which each event took place. You may wish to review the information in your textbook before you begin.

_____ Gold is discovered on Cherokee lands; settlers pour in to stake their claims.

_____ Chief Justice John Marshall gives the Court's ruling that the United States should protect the Cherokees and their lands in Georgia, but President Jackson ignores the ruling.

_____ Congress passes the Indian Removal Act, forcing all Indians living east of the Mississippi to move to the Indian Territory.

_____ The United States government agrees to accept the independence of the Cherokee nation.

_____ Andrew Jackson becomes the seventh President of the United States.

_____ A large group of Cherokees begin the journey that has come to be known as the Trail of Tears; more than 4,000 Cherokees die.

DIRECTIONS: Use the information above to complete the following activities.

1. Circle the date of the event that marks the beginning of forced relocation of native peoples from the East to the West.

2. Underline an economic reason why the Cherokees were forced from their lands.

3. Draw a box around the year that marks the beginning of the Trail of Tears.

4. On a separate sheet of paper, draw a horizontal time line using the dates and events listed above. Start your time line at 1790 and end it at 1840. Make one inch represent a ten-year period.

NAME _____ DATE _____

THE Oregon Trail

Arrange Information in Order

DIRECTIONS: Read the following sentences about a trip on the Oregon Trail. Then place the sentences in the proper order by numbering them from 1 to 6, with 1 being the earliest event and 6 being the latest event.

_____ A steamboat carries our family up the river from St. Louis to Independence, Missouri.

_____ The wagons in our group finally arrive in Willamette Valley. Oregon at last!

_____ At nightfall the wagons in our group circle for camp.

_____ In Independence we load our possessions onto a wagon and hear the cry, "Wagons roll!"

_____ We leave our home in the East and board a train headed for St. Louis, Missouri.

_____ In the morning we eat breakfast, and then continue our journey by wagon to Oregon.

DIRECTIONS: Study the list of supplies below. Then complete the activities that follow.

One box of sardines	$16	_____
One pound of hard bread	$ 2	_____
One pound of butter	$ 6	_____
One-half pound of cheese	$ 3	_____
Total	_____	

1. Number the items from most expensive to least expensive in the spaces provided. Start numbering with *1* as the most expensive.

2. Write the total cost of the supplies in the space provided.

3. Imagine that you can spend only $25. Put a line through the item or items that you would have to take off your list.

NAME _____ DATE _____

HOW TO USE RELIEF and Elevation Maps

Apply Map and Globe Skills

DIRECTIONS: Study the map of the Oregon Trail. Then answer the questions that follow.

1. Write in the correct sequence the names of the physical features you would pass through if you traveled the Oregon Trail from Independence, Missouri, to Fort Vancouver.

   _____
   _____
   _____

2. Trace over the part of the Oregon Trail that passes through the Rocky Mountains.

   Through which forts does this part of the trail pass? _____

3. Which river did the Oregon Trail follow just west of the Rocky Mountains?

   _____

4. On a separate sheet of paper, describe the trip along the Oregon Trail from Independence to Portland. Include in your description the forts and landmarks along the way and the changes in the geography.

80 ACTIVITY BOOK   Use after reading Chapter 12, Skill Lesson, pages 452–453.

NAME _____ DATE _____

Seneca Falls

Compare Primary Sources

DIRECTIONS: Read the following opening lines of the Declaration of Sentiments by Elizabeth Cady Stanton. Complete the activities that follow by comparing these lines with the opening lines of the Declaration of Independence which can be found on page R19 in your textbook.

Declaration of Sentiments

When, in the course of human events, it becomes necessary for one portion of the family of man to assume among the people of the earth a position different from that which they have hitherto occupied, but one to which the laws of nature and of nature's God entitle them, a decent respect to the opinions of mankind requires that they should declare the causes that impel them to such a course.

We hold these truths to be self-evident: that all men and women are created equal; that they are endowed by their Creator with certain inalienable rights; that among these are life, liberty, and the pursuit of happiness. . . .

1. Underline the words in the Declaration of Sentiments that are different from the words in the Declaration of Independence.

2. Why do you think the author of this document did not change the word "mankind"?

_____
_____
_____

3. Write the phrase from the Declaration of Independence that was completely left out of the Declaration of Sentiments. (Don't include words used as substitutes.)

_____
_____
_____

4. Why do you think the author would model the Declaration of Sentiments after the Declaration of Independence?

_____
_____
_____

Use after reading Chapter 12, Lesson 4, pages 454–458.

HOW TO USE A Double-Bar Graph

Apply Chart and Graph Skills

DIRECTIONS: Use the facts at the right to make a double-bar graph in the space below. Create a key and title for your graph. Then answer the questions on the next page.

POPULATION GROWTH 1790–1860 (IN THOUSANDS)		
YEAR	AFRICAN	WHITE
1790	757	3,172
1800	1,002	4,306
1810	1,378	5,862
1820	1,772	7,867
1830	2,329	10,537
1840	2,874	14,196
1850	3,639	19,553
1860	4,442	26,923

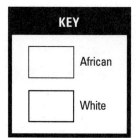

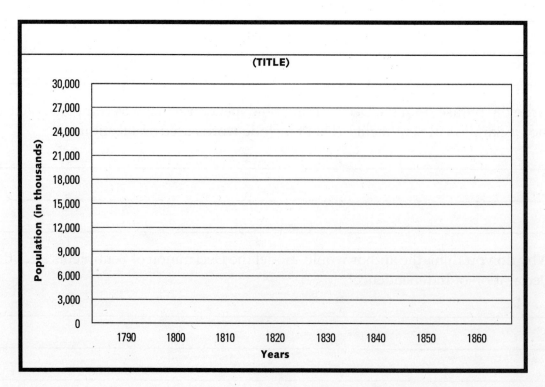

(continued)

NAME _____ DATE _____

1. What interval is used on the bar graph to show the increase in population?
   _____

2. What interval is used to show the passage of time? _____

3. How many years of data does this bar graph cover? _____

4. During which ten-year period did the white population grow the least?
   _____

5. During which ten-year period was there the least growth in the African population?
   _____

6. Compare the growth of the African population with that of the white population. List two generalizations you can make using the data.

   _____
   _____
   _____
   _____
   _____
   _____

7. Compare the table on page 82 with the double-bar graph you created. Which of the two makes it easier for you to understand the information? Why?

   _____
   _____
   _____
   _____
   _____
   _____

Use after reading Chapter 12, Skill Lesson, page 459.

NAME _____ DATE _____

THE WAY WEST

Connect Main Ideas

DIRECTIONS: Use this organizer to show how the chapter's main ideas are connected. Write three details to support each main idea.

The Industrial Revolution
New technology changed life in the United States in the 1800s.

1. _____
2. _____
3. _____

The Age of Jackson
Problems divided the American people in the early 1800s.

1. _____
2. _____
3. _____

The Way West

Westward Ho!
The United States expanded its territory in the 1800s.

1. _____
2. _____
3. _____

An Age of Reform
People in the 1800s worked to make American society better.

1. _____
2. _____
3. _____

Use after reading Chapter 12, pages 430–461.

NAME _____ DATE _____

A TALE OF TWO REGIONS 1860

Analyze Information in a Table

DIRECTIONS: The table below compares the North with the South in 1860. Use the information in your textbook to complete the table. Then answer the questions that follow to show that you understand how the two regions differed.

TWO WAYS OF LIFE: 1860

	NORTH	SOUTH
Total Number of People		
Number of Enslaved People		
Number of Factories	119,500	20,850
Number of Factory Workers	1,300,000	110,000
Annual Value of Factory Products	$1,730,000,000	$156,000,000
Miles of Railroad Track	21,500	8,500
Value of Exports	$175,000,000	$226,000,000
Money in Banks	$345,900,000	$76,000,000

1. List three details from the table that support the idea that there was more manufacturing in the North than in the South.

_____

_____

_____

2. List one detail from the table that supports the idea that the South relied on trade with other countries more than the North did. _____

_____

3. Which region had more miles of railroad track? _____
How might having more miles of railroad track affect that region's economy?

_____

_____

Use after reading Chapter 13, Lesson 1, pages 477–482.

NAME _____ DATE _____

How To Use Graphs To Identify Trends

In the early 1800s most people in both the North and the South lived and worked on farms. Today, farming continues to be an important economic activity throughout much of the United States. However, the number of farms has changed greatly over time.

Year	Number of Farms
1850	1,500,000
1880	4,000,000
1920	6,500,000
1980	2,400,000
1992	2,100,000

Apply Chart and Graph Skills

DIRECTIONS: Use the facts at the right to make a line graph in the space below. Add a title to your graph. Then answer the questions that follow.

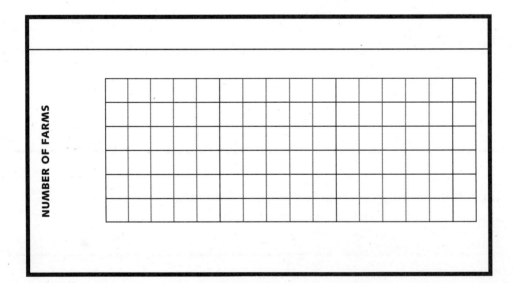

1. What was the trend between 1850 and 1920? _____

2. What was the trend between 1920 and 1992? _____

3. How would you explain the trends? _____

_____

_____

86 ACTIVITY BOOK   Use after reading Chapter 13, Skill Lesson, page 483.

NAME _____ DATE _____

THE LIFE AND TIMES OF A SLAVE

Gather Information in Reference Books

DIRECTIONS: Read the passage from Frederick Douglass's *autobiography*, The Life and Times of Frederick Douglass.

My first experience of life, as I now remember it, began in the family of my grandmother and grandfather, Betsey and Isaac Bailey. . . .

. . . Whether because she [Grandmother Betsey] was too old for field service, or because she had so faithfully done the duties of her station in early life, I know not, but she enjoyed the special right of living in a cabin separate from the other cabins, having given her only the charge of the young children and the burden of her support. . . . The practice of separating mothers from their children and hiring them out at distances too great to allow their meeting, except after long periods of time, was a marked feature of the cruelty and hardness of the slave system. . . .

My grandmother's five daughters were hired out . . . and my only recollections of my own mother are of a few hasty visits made in the night on foot, after the daily tasks were over, and when she had to return in time to answer the driver's call to the field in the early morning. These little glimpses of my mother under such conditions and against such odds, meager as they were, are permanently stamped upon my memory. She was tall and had dark, glossy skin with regular features, and amongst the slaves was remarkably sedate and dignified.

DIRECTIONS: Use the passage above and other available resources to answer the following questions about Frederick Douglass on a separate sheet of paper. For each question, tell whether you used only the passage to find the answer or whether you needed to use an encyclopedia, a dictionary, or some other reference book.

1. When was Frederick Douglass born, and when did he die?

2. In what state did Douglass live as a slave?

3. Who raised Douglass as a boy?

4. How did Douglass describe his mother?

Use after reading Chapter 13, Lesson 2, pages 484–489.

NAME _____ DATE _____

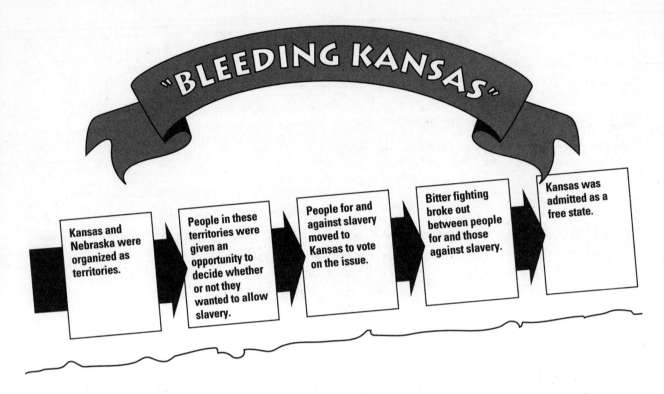

Expand Thinking About an Issue

DIRECTIONS: Use the flow chart above and the information in your textbook to answer the questions below.

1. How did the Kansas–Nebraska Act deal with the spread of slavery?

   _____

2. How do you think people in the North reacted to the Kansas–Nebraska Act?

   _____

3. How do you think people in the South viewed the Kansas–Nebraska Act?

   _____

4. What were the major effects of the Kansas–Nebraska Act in Kansas?

   _____

5. Why did Southern states begin to talk more about secession after Kansas became a state?

   _____
   _____

6. Do you think the Kansas–Nebraska Act was a good law? Why or why not?

   _____

NAME _____ DATE _____

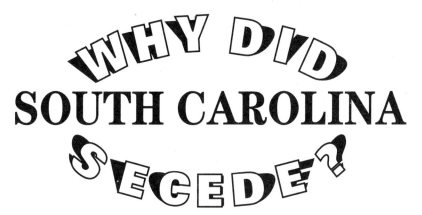

Recognize Point of View

DIRECTIONS: Read the following paragraph from the South Carolina Secession Ordinance of December 20, 1860.

SOUTH CAROLINA SECESSION ORDINANCE
December 20, 1860

An agreement between the states set up a government with specific purposes and powers. We feel that the reasons for which this government was begun have been defeated. The government itself has destroyed them by the action of the Northern, nonslaveholding states. **(1)** Those states have assumed the right to decide the properness of our domestic practices (that is, slavery). **(2)** They have denied our rights of property recognized by the Constitution. They have denounced as sinful the practice of slavery. **(3)** They have permitted the organization of abolitionist groups, whose goal is to disturb the peace of and to take away the property of the citizens of our states. **(4)** Those groups have encouraged and helped thousands of our slaves to leave their homes; and the slaves who remain have been incited by special agents, books, and pictures into insurrection.

DIRECTIONS: For each numbered sentence in the South Carolina Secession Ordinance, state in your own words a South Carolina complaint from a Southern point of view. Then write a response that tells a Northern point of view. Use your textbook if you need more information.

Southern Complaint		Northern Response
1. _____	▷	_____
2. _____	▷	_____
3. _____	▷	_____
4. _____	▷	_____

Use after reading Chapter 13, Lesson 4, pages 496–500.

NAME _____ DATE _____

HOW TO MAKE A THOUGHTFUL DECISION

Apply Critical Thinking Skills

DIRECTIONS: Think about a decision you made recently at school, or think about a decision that someone made during the Civil War. Then use the organizer below to record and analyze that decision. Fill in as many possible actions and consequences as you can.

THE GOAL

POSSIBLE ACTIONS	POSSIBLE CONSEQUENCES
1. _____	1. _____
2. _____	2. _____
3. _____	3. _____
4. _____	4. _____

THE CHOICE	REASONS FOR THE CHOICE

THE RESULT

NAME _____ DATE _____

Background to the CONFLICT

Connect Main Ideas

DIRECTIONS: Use this organizer to show how the chapter's main ideas are connected. Write three details to support each main idea.

Differences Divide North and South
People in the North and the South disagreed during the mid-1800s.

1. _____
2. _____
3. _____

Africans in Slavery and Freedom
Enslaved people protested being held in slavery.

1. _____
2. _____
3. _____

Background to the Conflict

Facing a National Problem
Northerners and Southerners tried to settle disagreements during the 1800s.

1. _____
2. _____
3. _____

A Time for Hard Decisions
Americans had to make important decisions in 1860 and 1861.

1. _____
2. _____
3. _____

Use after reading Chapter 13, pages 476–505.

NAME _____ DATE _____

THE BONNIE BLUE FLAG

When South Carolina joined the Confederacy, its flag changed, but Harry Macarthy's song, "The Bonnie Blue Flag," which was about South Carolina's first flag, quickly became the Confederacy's national anthem.

Link Music to History

DIRECTIONS: Read the words to the song. Then answer the questions that follow.

Verse One
1. We are a band of brothers, and native to the soil,
2. Fighting for the property we gained by honest toil;
3. And when our rights were threatened, the cry rose near and far:
4. Hurrah! for the bonnie blue flag that bears a single star.

Verse Two
1. As long as the Union was faithful to her trust,
2. Like friends and like brothers, kind were we and just;
3. But now, when Northern treachery attempts our rights to mar,
4. We hoist, on high, the bonnie blue flag that bears a single star.

Last Verse
1. Then here's to our Confederacy—strong we are and brave,
2. Like patriots of old, we'll fight, our heritage to save;
3. And rather than submit to shame, to die we would prefer—
4. So cheer for the bonnie blue flag that bears a single star.

Chorus
1. Hurrah! hurrah! for Southern rights! hurrah!
2. Hurrah! for the bonnie blue flag that bears a single star.

1. Write the phrase that is repeated in line 4 of each verse.

_____

2. Which line in Verse One describes how the Confederate soldiers felt about one another? Describe that feeling. _____

_____

3. Each verse has one line that states a reason that the Confederacy was fighting. List each line number and give the reason.

Verse One   Line Number: _____   Reason: _____

Verse Two   Line Number: _____   Reason: _____

Last Verse   Line Number: _____   Reason: _____

92 ACTIVITY BOOK   Use after reading Chapter 14, Lesson 1, pages 507–513.

NAME _____ DATE _____

THE Emancipation Proclamation

Interpret Primary Source Documents

DIRECTIONS: The passage below from the Emancipation Proclamation contains words in boldface type. Use context clues to define those words. Match each word in the list with its definition, and write the correct letter in the blank. Then, on a separate sheet of paper, answer the questions that follow.

And by **virtue** of the power and for the purpose **aforesaid,** I do order and declare that all persons held as slaves within said **designated** States and parts of States are, and **henceforward** shall be, free; and that the Executive Government of the United States, including the military and naval authorities thereof, will recognize and maintain the freedom of said persons.

And I hereby enjoin upon the people so declared to be free to **abstain** from all violence, unless in necessary self-defense; and I recommend to them that, in all cases when allowed, they labor faithfully for reasonable wages.

And I further declare and make known that such persons of **suitable** condition will be received into the armed service of the United States to **garrison** forts, positions, stations, and other places, and to **man** vessels of all sorts in said service.

_____ virtue   **A.** pointed out; shown

_____ aforesaid   **B.** from this time on

_____ designated   **C.** because of; on the grounds of

_____ henceforward   **D.** right; proper

_____ abstain   **E.** spoken of before; mentioned previously

_____ suitable   **F.** to station troops in a fort or town

_____ garrison   **G.** to take an assigned place for work or defense

_____ man   **H.** to keep oneself back; to choose not to do

1. What is the most important message in the first paragraph?

2. What did President Lincoln recommend to former slaves in the second paragraph?

3. In the last paragraph, what did President Lincoln declare about the armed services?

Use after reading Chapter 14, Lesson 2, pages 514–519.

NAME _____   DATE _____

★ CIVIL WAR ★ HORSES

Apply Information from a Chart

DIRECTIONS: Study the chart below. Then complete the activities that follow.

CIVIL WAR GENERALS' HORSES

HORSE'S NAME	RIDER'S NAME	ARMY	DESCRIPTION	FURTHERMORE
Don Juan	George Armstrong Custer	Union	Bay stallion	Custer had more horses (7) killed under him than any other Union leader.
Butler	Wade Hampton	Confederate	Bay stallion	One of Hampton's officers gave him the horse as a gift.
Sam	William Tecumseh Sherman	Union	Half-breed bay stallion	The horse was so steady under gunfire that Sherman could write orders while riding.
Lexington	William Tecumseh Sherman	Union	Kentucky thoroughbred	Sherman rode Lexington during his final review of his army.
Traveller	Robert E. Lee	Confederate	Iron gray gelding	Traveller was called the greatest warhorse of all time, except for Alexander the Great's horse.
Old Spot	Judson Kilpatrick	Union	Arabian	The horse outlived his master.

1. Underline the name of the general who had seven horses killed under him.

2. Put a star next to the name of each general who rode a bay stallion.

3. Put a box around the name of the horse that outlived his master.

4. a) Imagine you are a Civil War general. Explain why it is important to choose a good horse.

_____
_____
_____

b) Which of the horses on the chart would you have chosen? Explain your answer.

_____
_____
_____

NAME _____ DATE _____

HOW TO COMPARE MAPS with DIFFERENT SCALES

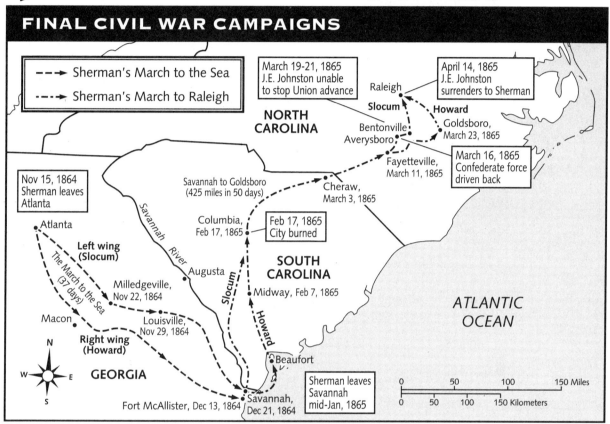

Apply Map and Globe Skills

DIRECTIONS: Compare the map above with the map in your textbook on page 525. For each of the following statements, decide which map is more useful. Write **A** in the answer blank if the map above is better and **B** if the textbook map is better.

_____ 1. Show the most miles per inch.

_____ 2. Determine the distance between Cheraw and Fayetteville.

_____ 3. Determine how many miles Sherman traveled on his March to the Sea.

_____ 4. Identify the extent of the Union blockade.

_____ 5. Measure the distance from Atlanta, Georgia, to Macon, Georgia.

_____ 6. Identify battles that took place in Mississippi and Virginia.

_____ 7. Determine the number of miles traveled by Sherman's army between February 17, 1865, and March 11, 1865.

Use after reading Chapter 14, Skill Lesson, pages 528–529.

IT'S IN THE BAG!

Interpret Visuals and Point of View

DIRECTIONS: Study the illustrations and the captions below. Then on a separate sheet of paper, answer the questions that follow.

After the Civil War inexpensive suitcases called carpetbags (above) were made from carpeting.

THE MAN WITH THE (CARPET) BAGS
Cartoonist Thomas Nast helped shape the U.S. public's view of Reconstruction. This 1872 cartoon shows a former Union general.

1. Circle the name of the Union general in Nast's cartoon.

2. Underline the direction in which the general is heading.

3. Compare the bags in the cartoon with the one in the illustration next to the cartoon. What similarities and differences do you notice?

4. Look at the illustration on the left. How do you think this type of bag got its name?

5. How do you think Nast viewed the type of person in this cartoon? List the features of this cartoon that support your answer.

6. Nast said about this cartoon, "The bag in front of him, filled with others' faults, he always sees. The one behind him, filled with his own faults, he never sees." Explain what you think Nast meant.

NAME _____ DATE _____

Civil War and Reconstruction

Connect Main Ideas

DIRECTIONS: Use this organizer to show how the chapter's main ideas are connected. Write a sentence or two telling how each event or idea affected the lives of Americans during the Civil War and Reconstruction.

Choosing Sides

Emancipation Proclamation

Civil War and Reconstruction

Union Victories

Rebuilding America

Use after reading Chapter 14, pages 506–539.

NAME _____ DATE _____

Famous Entrepreneurs

Categorize Information

DIRECTIONS: Read the stories that follow, and use the information to fill in the chart. Use your textbook and library reference materials to fill in the information about Andrew Carnegie.

Levi Strauss, a Jewish immigrant from Germany, left New York City for the West in 1850. He went west to sell canvas to settlers to use for sails and coverings for their wagons. When he arrived there, he found that settlers could not find pants strong enough to last. Strauss took his canvas material and made it into the first pair of jeans. His company became Levi Strauss & Co.

John Harvey Kellogg, of British ancestry, believed that a healthful diet would help people heal more quickly from illness. He was once sued by an elderly woman who broke her false teeth on a zwieback (hard bread) that he had recommended for her to eat. As a result of this incident, he started to think about producing a softer ready-to-eat food. One night he dreamed of how to make flaked foods. This dream resulted in his producing the first dry cereal, which today is known as Kellogg's Cornflakes.

Fannie Merritt Farmer was born in Boston of British descent. She suffered a childhood illness that left her with a limp. After doctors discouraged her from going to college, she entered cooking school in 1887. By 1891 she was running it! In those days, cooking ingredients were measured by "pinches and dabs." Farmer applied science to cooking. In her best-selling cookbook, she standardized measurements. You can thank her for the level teaspoon.

FAMOUS ENTREPRENEURS			
ENTREPRENEUR	HERITAGE	COMPANY/PRODUCT	FUN FACT
Levi Strauss			
John Harvey Kellogg			
Fannie Merritt Farmer			
Andrew Carnegie			

NAME _____ DATE _____

HOW TO USE A Time Zone MAP

Apply Map and Globe Skills

DIRECTIONS: Study the time zone map below. The clock in the eastern time zone is set at 11:00 A.M. Draw the hands on the clocks in the other time zones, and note whether the time shown is A.M. or P.M. Then use different colors to shade in the time zones on the map and the key.

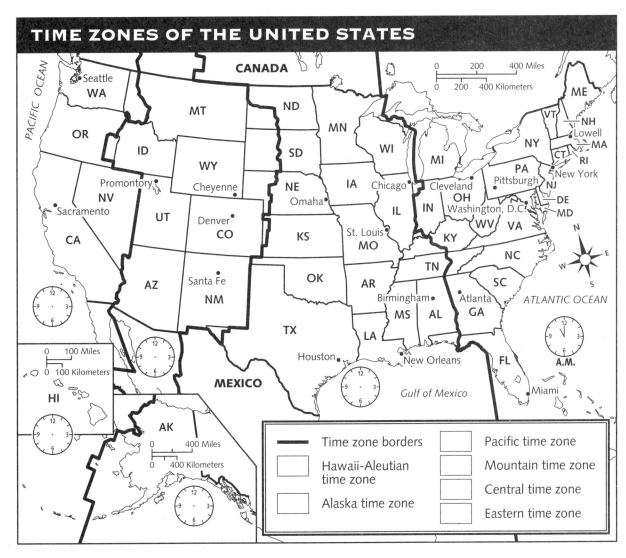

(continued)

Use after reading Chapter 15, Skill Lesson, pages 560–561.

ACTIVITY BOOK 99

NAME _____ DATE _____

DIRECTIONS: Study the time zone map on page 99. Complete the activities that follow.

1. How many time zones are located in the United States? _____

2. In which time zone is your city located? _____

3. In which time zones are the following cities located:

   Chicago, Illinois _____   St. Louis, Missouri _____

   Cleveland, Ohio _____   Atlanta, Georgia _____

4. Andrew Carnegie produced his steel in Pittsburgh, Pennsylvania. If he transported it by railroad from Pittsburgh to the West Coast, through how many time zones would the steel travel? _____

5. John D. Rockefeller set up an oil refinery in Cleveland, Ohio. He later bought refineries in West Virginia. If he traveled from his refinery in Ohio to his refinery in West Virginia, through how many time zones would he travel? _____

   _____

6. The Union Pacific Railroad built west from Omaha, Nebraska. The Central Pacific Railroad built east from Sacramento, California.

   A. If it is 7:00 P.M. in Sacramento, what time is it in Omaha? _____

   B. If it is 8:00 A.M. in Omaha, what time is it in Sacramento? _____

7. The two railroads met at Promontory, Utah. If it is 10 A.M. in Promontory,

   A. What time is it in Omaha? _____

   B. What time is it in Sacramento? _____

8. If the Super Bowl aired on TV from New Orleans at 3:00 P.M., what time would sports fans in Hawaii have to turn on their television sets to see the game? _____

9. Imagine you live in Denver, Colorado, and have a scheduled school lunch at noon.

   A. What time would it be in our nation's capital? _____

   B. What do you think students in the nation's capital would be doing at that time?

   _____

   _____

100 ACTIVITY BOOK   Use after reading Chapter 15, Skill Lesson, pages 560–561.

NAME _____ DATE _____

Duke Ellington

Interpret Information

DIRECTIONS: Read the paragraph below about one of the world's greatest jazz musicians, Duke Ellington. Then answer the questions that follow.

Duke Ellington was born in 1899 in Washington, D.C. He wrote music, led bands, and played the piano. In the 1920s he moved to Harlem, in New York City, to be a part of the large and growing African American community of artists and musicians living there. His band played in concert halls and theaters all over the world. Duke Ellington wrote more than 1,500 songs, including music for Broadway plays and motion pictures. Much of his music is now part of the Duke Ellington Collection at the Smithsonian Institution in Washington, D.C.

1. Why did Duke Ellington want to move to Harlem?

_____

_____

2. How did inventions like the phonograph and the radio help Duke Ellington and his band become known by many people?

_____

_____

3. Duke Ellington wrote music for plays and motion pictures. What changes in American life do you think gave people more time to enjoy plays and motion pictures?

_____

_____

4. Why do you think it's important that much of Duke Ellington's music is part of the Duke Ellington Collection at the Smithsonian Institution in Washington, D.C.?

_____

_____

Use after reading Chapter 15, Lesson 2, pages 562–567.

NAME _____ DATE _____

ORGANIZING Resources

Understand Economics

DIRECTIONS: Three kinds of resources are needed to make a product: natural resources, or raw materials, such as minerals and ores; capital resources, such as money, tools, and equipment; and human resources, or workers. Conduct library research and complete the organizer below to show what resources are needed to make each product listed in the center box.

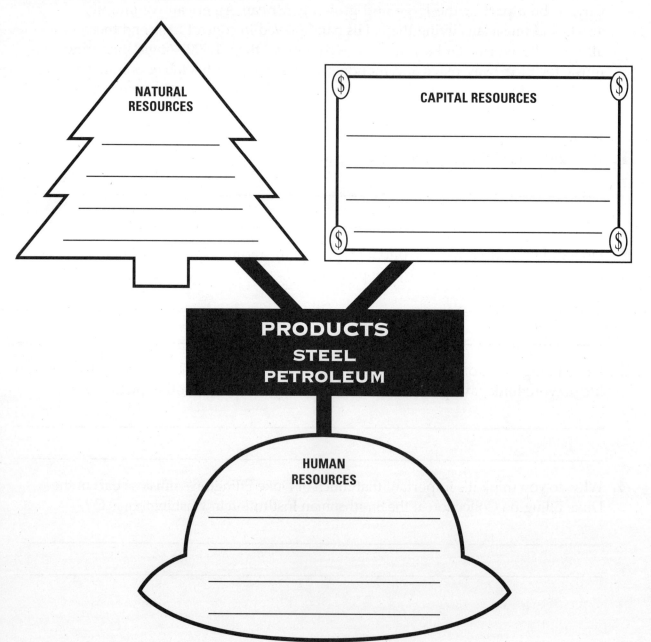

102   ACTIVITY BOOK

Use after reading Chapter 15, Lesson 3, pages 568–573.

NAME _____ DATE _____

School Days

Relate Past to Present

DIRECTIONS: *The following excerpt from* Immigrant Kids *by Russell Freedman describes a typical school day in New York City in the early 1900s. Read the excerpt. Then answer the questions that follow.*

When teacher called out in her sharp, penetrating voice, "Class!" everyone sat up straight as a ramrod, eyes front, hands clasped rigidly behind one's back. We strived painfully to please her. With a thin smile of approval on her face, her eyes roved over the stiff, rigid figures in front of her.

Beautiful script letters across the huge blackboard and a chart of the alphabet were the sole adornments of the classroom. Every day the current lesson from our speller was meticulously written out on the blackboard by the teacher. . . . We spent hours over our copybooks, all conveniently lined, as we laboriously sought to imitate this perfection.

We had to learn our lessons by heart, and we repeated them out loud until we memorized them. Playgrounds were nonexistent, toilets were in the yard, and gymnasiums were an unheard-of luxury.

1. Use context clues to define *penetrating*. _____

2. Use context clues to describe your image of a ramrod. _____

_____

_____

3. Compare the adornments, or decorations, in the classroom described with the ones in

your classroom. _____

_____

4. Describe differences between the way the teacher presented lessons in the early 1900s and the way your teacher presents lessons. Include descriptions of methods and materials.

_____

_____

5. On a separate sheet of paper, write three paragraphs about your school, using the above three paragraphs as a guide. Describe the same things described in each paragraph, but use your school and class as the topic.

NAME _____ DATE _____

HOW TO SOLVE A PROBLEM

Apply Critical Thinking Skills

DIRECTIONS: Choose a problem in your school, such as one related to school lunches, bus schedules, or class size. Use the flow chart below to suggest a solution. You may copy the flow chart onto a separate sheet of paper if necessary.

Decide what the problem is. List the problem.
_____
_____

Think of possible solutions. List the solutions.
_____
_____
_____

Think about the possible results of each solution. List the possible results of each solution.
_____
_____
_____

Choose one solution. List this solution.
_____
_____
_____

Think about how well your solution solves the problem. Explain how your solution solves the problem.
_____
_____
_____

Use after reading Chapter 15, Skill Lesson, page 579.

NAME _____ DATE _____

A Changing America

Connect Main Ideas

DIRECTIONS: Use this organizer to show how the chapter's main ideas are connected. Complete the organizer by writing two or three sentences that summarize the main idea of each lesson.

Big Business and Industrial Cities

_____
_____
_____
_____
_____

Inventions Change Daily Life

_____
_____
_____
_____
_____

A Changing America

Growing Pains

_____
_____
_____
_____
_____
_____
_____

The Growth of Cities

_____
_____
_____
_____
_____
_____
_____

Use after reading Chapter 15, pages 554–581.

Immigration

Distinguish Fact from Opinion

DIRECTIONS: Study the quotations below, which were made by immigrants who came to the United States at the beginning of the twentieth century. Then decide which of the following statements is fact and which is opinion. Write an F next to the statements of fact. Write an O next to the statements of opinion.

> As far as Ellis Island was concerned, it was a nightmare. After all, none of us spoke English.
> — *Nina Goodenov*

> The examiner [at Ellis Island] sat bureaucratically . . . I was questioned as to the state of my finances and I produced the required twenty-five dollars.
> — *Louis Adamic*

> We lived there [Ellis Island] for three days . . . Because of the rigorous physical examination that we had to submit to, particularly of the eyes, there was this terrible anxiety that one of us might be rejected.
> — *Angelo Pellegrini*

> America is . . . the great Melting Pot where all the races of Europe are melting and re-forming.
> — *Israel Zangwill*

_____ 1. Ellis Island was a nightmare.

_____ 2. Immigrants were required to produce $25 to enter the United States.

_____ 3. Immigrants had to take a physical examination.

_____ 4. The examiner at Ellis Island was unfriendly.

_____ 5. America is a great Melting Pot.

_____ 6. Immigrants who were not in good physical health could be rejected from the United States.

_____ 7. Some immigrants had to spend several days waiting on Ellis Island.

_____ 8. Many immigrants could not speak English.

NAME _____ DATE _____

HOW TO COMPARE Information on Graphs

Apply Chart and Graph Skills

DIRECTIONS: Use the information in the bar graph and the circle graph below to answer the questions that follow.

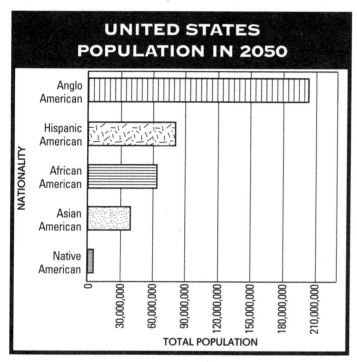
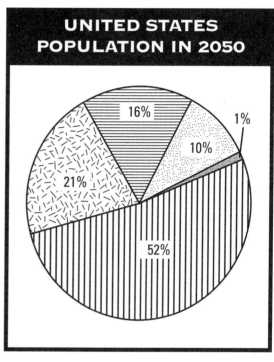

1. Which graph would you use to find the total number of Asian Americans living in the United States in 2050? _____

2. What will be the percentage of Asian Americans and African Americans in the United States in 2050? _____ Which graph did you use to find the percentage of Asian Americans and African Americans? _____

3. Which nationality will make up the second-largest percentage of the population in 2050? _____

4. Which nationality will have a population of about 40,000,000 in 2050? _____

5. What will be the percentage of Native Americans in the United States in 2050? _____ Does this percentage represent more than or less than 30,000,000 people? _____

Use after reading Chapter 16, Skill Lesson, pages 590–591.

AN African American PORTRAIT

Read a Table

DIRECTIONS: Study this table, which shows what percentage of the African American population lived in different regions of the United States during different time periods. Look for patterns. Then complete the activities that follow.

AFRICAN AMERICANS IN THE UNITED STATES, BY REGION (in percentages)

YEAR	NORTHEAST	NORTH CENTRAL	SOUTH	WEST
1860	3.5	4.1	92.2	0.1
1870	3.7	5.6	90.6	0.1
1880	3.5	5.9	90.5	0.2
1890	3.6	5.8	90.3	0.4
1900	4.4	5.6	89.7	0.3
1910	4.9	5.5	89.0	0.5
1920	6.5	7.6	85.2	0.8
1930	9.6	10.6	78.7	1.0

1. In which region did the percentage of African Americans decrease steadily from 1860 to 1930? _____

2. In which region did the percentage of African Americans increase the most from 1860 to 1930? What was the amount of percentage increase in this region?

3. During which ten-year period did the percentage of African Americans living in the South decrease the most? How much of a decrease was there during this period?

4. Migration was one reason that the percentage of African Americans in the South decreased during this time. Reread Jacob Lawrence's *The Great Migration: An American Story* in your textbook. Look for reasons that African Americans migrated. Copy the following headings onto a separate sheet of paper, and use information from the story to complete a chart showing reasons for African American migration.

FACTORS PUSHING AFRICAN AMERICANS OUT OF THE SOUTH	FACTORS PULLING AFRICAN AMERICANS TO OTHER REGIONS

NAME _____ DATE _____

Sing About CIVIL RIGHTS

Link Music to History

DIRECTIONS: Read the words to the following civil rights song "If You Miss Me from the Back of the Bus." Then answer the questions and complete the activities that follow.

If you miss me from the back of the bus,
And you can't find me nowhere,
Come on up to the front of the bus,
I'll be riding up there,
I'll be riding up there,
I'll be riding up there.
Come on up to the front of the bus,
I'll be riding up there.

If you miss me from the front of the bus,
And you can't find me nowhere,
Come on up to the driver's seat,
I'll be drivin' up there.
I'll be drivin' up there,
I'll be drivin' up there,
Come on up to the driver's seat,
I'll be drivin' up there.

1. Who does "me" represent in the song? _____

2. Circle the words that describe the part of the bus where members of this group were <u>first</u> required to sit. Why did they sit there? _____
_____

3. In the second verse of the song, who is in the driver's seat?
_____

4. What is the purpose of this protest song? _____
_____
_____

5. Describe in your own words what civil rights mean to you. _____
_____
_____
_____

Use after reading Chapter 16, Lesson 3, pages 598–605.

NAME _____ DATE _____

HOW TO ACT AS A RESPONSIBLE CITIZEN

Citizens of the United States have certain rights that are guaranteed by the Constitution. However, people have to help protect these rights by being responsible citizens.

Apply Participation Skills

DIRECTIONS: Several rights of United States citizens are listed below. For each right, write two ways that people can be responsible citizens and protect their rights.

Right: Freedom of speech

    Responsibility 1: _____

    Responsibility 2: _____

Right: Freedom to gather in groups

    Responsibility 1: _____

    Responsibility 2: _____

Right: Voting

    Responsibility 1: _____

    Responsibility 2: _____

Right: Being a member of a jury trial

    Responsibility 1: _____

    Responsibility 2: _____

Right: Holding public office

    Responsibility 1: _____

    Responsibility 2: _____

NAME _____ DATE _____

An American Song

A song that tells of the beauty of America is "My Country 'Tis of Thee." The words to the song were written in 1831 by the Reverend Samuel F. Smith. Read the first two verses of the song.

My country, 'tis of thee,
Sweet Land of Liberty,
  Of thee I sing;
Land where my fathers died,
Land of the pilgrims' pride,
From every mountain side
  Let Freedom ring.

My native country, thee,
Land of the noble free, —
  Thy name I love;
I love thy rocks and rills,
Thy woods and templed hills,
My heart with rapture thrills
  Like that above.

Identify and Interpret Patriotic Songs

DIRECTIONS: Below are some lines from the song. For each line, write what you think the words mean or draw a picture that illustrates the meaning of the words.

1. "Sweet Land of Liberty,"

2. "Land of the pilgrims' pride,"

3. "I love thy rocks and rills [brooks],"

4. "Thy woods and templed hills,"

Use after reading Chapter 16, Lesson 4, pages 607–609.

NAME _____ DATE _____

The Promise of America

Connect Main Ideas

DIRECTIONS: Use this organizer to show how the chapter's main ideas are connected. Write three details to support each main idea.

The Promise of America

Immigrants in the United States faced problems.

1. _____
2. _____
3. _____

African Americans shared problems with other newcomers to cities.

1. _____
2. _____
3. _____

Individuals worked to improve life in the United States in the twentieth century.

1. _____
2. _____
3. _____

Citizens of the United States contribute to their communities and our nation as a whole.

1. _____
2. _____
3. _____